R.B. OUELLETTE

UNDER PRESSURE

Overcoming Seasons of Stress with Biblical Wisdom

A previous edition of this book was published in 2008 by
Sword of the Lord Publishers under the title *Crunch Time*.
This updated and edited edition was first published in 2018 by
Striving Together Publications, a ministry of Lancaster Baptist
Church, Lancaster, CA 93535. Striving Together Publications
is committed to providing tried, trusted, and proven books
that will further equip local churches to carry out the Great
Commission. Your comments and suggestions are valued.

Striving Together Publications
4020 E. Lancaster Blvd.
Lancaster, CA 93535
800.201.7748

The author and publication team have given every effort to
give proper credit to quotes and thoughts that are not original
with the author. It is not our intent to claim originality with
any quote or thought that could not readily be tied to an
original source.

ISBN 978-1-59894-381-8
Printed in the United States of America

DEDICATION

This book is dedicated with love to our daughter, Karissa, her husband, Thomas Coats, and their children, Ashley, Ethan, and Amari. It is a delight to watch you serve the Lord together in the ministry. I love you.

CONTENTS

PRESSURE AS A PART OF LIFE

In one of the deadliest shootings in American history, Seung-Hui Cho opened fire on the campus of Virginia Tech University on April 16, 2007. At the end of his deadly spree, thirty-two were dead and many more injured. In the middle of the tragedy, however, everyday heroes began to emerge. One man in particular stood out.

Liviu Librescu was a Holocaust survivor and one of the most respected teachers on the Virignia Tech campus. When Cho reached Librescu's classroom and began to break in, Librescu courageously blocked the door with his body, allowing several of his students to escape out the windows before the gunman killed him. Today, he is remembered as a hero for his courage under pressure.[1]

No one would have faulted Librescu for seeking safety in the midst of the shooting. He could have responded to the pressure by trying to escape, but instead, he placed himself directly in the path of the shooter to save the lives of his students.

We may never be in an extreme situation like Librescu was, but all of us will encounter seasons of pressure or stress. How we respond in these seasons has the power to influence the lives of others as well as our own.

Pressure comes in all shapes and sizes. It comes the moment you become a parent. You look down at your tiny miracle, wondering, "How do I raise this child?" It could come from a painful divorce or unexpected news you receive at a doctor's office. For many, pressure comes day-to-day as we try to balance budgets or pay off debts. Other times it comes in the form of a strong temptation, such as when Joseph was faced with Potiphar's wife.

In our sin-cursed world, pressure is a part of everyday life. And as the tension mounts, it can be hard to think clearly, let alone know how to respond. To compound the problem, the world offers conflicting advice. Do this. Don't do this. Whatever you do, make sure you respond like this.

---

[1] Marcus Barman, "Heroes in the Midst of Horror: Holocaust Survivor, Student Saved Others," *Abcnews.go.com*, April 17, 2007, https://abcnews.go.com/US/story?id=3049678&page=1 (accessed October 17, 2018).

And then your friends chime in. Well-meaning as they may be, they haven't been in your situation. It's hard for them to empathize with what you're going through, let alone show you the right thing to do. Sometimes, kind friends even offer advice that is not biblical.

Suddenly, you're not just facing a stressful situation; you're facing opposing opinions and options about what to do. The pressure is on, and you're starting to feel overwhelmed.

When we're under pressure, God wants us to run to Him for direction and comfort. The Psalmist wrote, "From the end of the earth will I cry unto thee, when my heart is overwhelmed: lead me to the rock that is higher than I" (Psalm 61:2).

In these pages, I invite you to explore with me what God's Word says about twelve specific seasons of stress you may encounter throughout your life. Ask God to speak to you as we look at what He says about real life problems. My prayer is that you'll come away from these chapters with a fresh perspective, armed with applicable, scriptural truths to help you face life's tensions head on. No matter what pressures life throws your way, there is hope.

You may not have personally experienced every season of pressure we discuss, but someone in your life or someone you meet may be dealing with one of these very issues. If they come to you for advice or counsel, you'll be glad you know what God's Word says about their problem, and you'll be better equipped to encourage them through their tough time.

When the pressure is on, we have God's Word to guide us, lead us, and direct us through it. And in the middle of the toughest seasons, we can have hope for the future.

PART ONE

FAMILIAR PRESSURES

ONE

DEALING WITH GRIEF

As a pastor, I've received many phone calls from people asking for prayer. I'll never forget one in particular. The person calling was a woman I had not met, but I could immediately tell she was hurting deeply. Her son, just sixteen years old, had been diagnosed with a brain tumor. He was left with only a short time to live.

Heartbroken, the mother cried on the other end of the phone, "O Lord, no! Take *me*, and let my son live."

I prayed with her and did my best to offer her encouragement and comfort from Scripture, but that experience early in my ministry indelibly etched one thing in my mind: it's difficult to know how to proceed in the face of grief. This is true whether you are the one grieving or the one trying to offer comfort.

Grief is universal. Since sin entered into the world through Adam, all of us have been subject to pain, broken hearts, and death (Romans 5:12). At some time in our lives, all of us will experience grief.

Why, then, if grief is so universal, is there so much confusion over what it is and how to biblically deal with it? I've spoken to some who seem to think that truly spiritual people don't grieve. Yet the Bible refers to Jesus as "a man of sorrows, and acquainted with grief" (Isaiah 53:3).

The Bible never guarantees we won't grieve, but there is an important distinction to make between our grief and the world's grief. As Christians, we can know the amazing comfort of God through the ministry of the Holy Spirit. The Holy Spirit is our Comforter (John 14:16), and 2 Corinthians 1:3–4 tells us that ours is the "...God of all comfort; Who comforteth us in all our tribulation...."

But what does that really mean? In the middle of a trial, how *do* we cope with grief? What should we do when a friend is diagnosed with cancer and is looking to us for help? Or how do we proceed when we receive news of an accident that claimed the life of a loved one? How do we receive God's comfort when we are walking through a difficult health trial? Although we know that God offers us His comfort and strength, it can be tough to reconcile the grief we feel with the promises we know. How do we take the truths from God's Word and apply them to our lives when we're dealing with grief?

Biblical Examples of Grief

There is no easy way to navigate something as messy as grief. But we are certainly not alone on this road. Throughout the pages of Scripture, we discover men and women who also experienced seasons of grief.

Jacob and Joseph—Joseph was his father Jacob's favorite child. As a result, Joseph's brothers hated him. Finally, their hatred grew to the point that they sold their brother into slavery. To cover their tracks, however, they dipped Joseph's coat of many colors, a special gift from Jacob, into animal blood, and told Jacob that they had found the coat. Their plan to deceive their father into thinking Joseph had died worked, and Jacob grieved the loss of his beloved son Joseph.

> *And Jacob rent his clothes, and put sackcloth upon his loins, and mourned for his son many days. And all his sons and all his daughters rose up to comfort him; but he refused to be comforted; and he said, For I will go down into the grave unto my son mourning. Thus his father wept for him.*
> —GENESIS 37:34–35

Jacob was so troubled that he tore his clothes and wore sackcloth, an uncomfortable fabric, to emphasize the magnitude of his grief. Clothing was difficult to make back then, and even a wealthy man like Jacob probably only had a few garments. Therefore, if a person rent his garments, he was under tremendous grief.

In Jacob's time, a typical mourning period lasted seven days. People would generally remain inside their homes, not even putting on their shoes, because they had no plans to leave. The Bible says that Jacob grieved the loss of his son for *many* days.

Maybe you've experienced the loss of someone close to you. The emotions and hurt you feel are real and painful. Jacob understood what that felt like.

Job and his family—Job could have related to Jacob's grief. In fact, if someone asked you to name Bible characters who endured many trials, Job would probably be at the top of your list. Think about it. All of his children died in one day; he lost many of his possessions; and then he endured debilitating, painful health issues. Job 1 records his grief:

> *Then Job arose, and rent his mantle, and shaved his head, and fell down upon the ground, and worshipped, And said, Naked came I out of my mother's womb, and naked shall I return thither: the LORD gave, and the LORD hath taken away; blessed be the*

name of the Lord. *In all this Job sinned not,
nor charged God foolishly.*—Job 1:20–22

The following chapter records Job's friends' response:

*Now when Job's three friends heard of all
this evil that was come upon him, they
came every one from his own place; Eliphaz
the Temanite, and Bildad the Shuhite, and
Zophar the Naamathite: for they had made
an appointment together to come to mourn
with him and to comfort him. And when
they lifted up their eyes afar off, and knew
him not, they lifted up their voice, and
wept; and they rent every one his mantle,
and sprinkled dust upon their heads toward
heaven. So they sat down with him upon
the ground seven days and seven nights, and
none spake a word unto him: for they saw
that his grief was very great.*—Job 2:11–13

For the moment, Job's friends said nothing to him in
his sorrow. They just sat with him. Their response is often
the best response we can have when comforting a grieving
friend. Many times, your presence will bring more comfort
than your words. In fact, if you read the rest of Job's story,
you'll see that problems quickly arose when his friends did
begin to speak.

Sometimes, we feel obligated to find "just the right words" for those that are grieving. But you're not expected to be the perfect grief counselor. Just by being there, you can bring comfort. In fact, when we begin searching for the perfect words, we can say things that aren't even supported by Scripture.

David, Saul, and Jonathan—For years, a jealous King Saul sought David's life. He was one of David's greatest enemies, but David refused to be an enemy of Saul. In fact, on two separate occasions, David had the chance to kill Saul, but David refused. Even though Saul had forced David to flee his home and live in the wilderness, David believed it was wrong for him to touch the Lord's anointed. This passage recounts David's reaction to Saul's death.

> *Then David took hold on his clothes, and rent them; and likewise all the men that were with him: And they mourned, and wept, and fasted until even, for Saul, and for Jonathan his son, and for the people of the LORD, and for the house of Israel; because they were fallen by the sword.*
> —2 SAMUEL 1:11–12

David's reaction is the opposite of what we could consider normal. Put yourself in David's place. The man that has relentlessly sought your life and forced you into hiding is now killed in battle. My first reaction would probably be to say something like, "Finally! God has avenged me and judged Saul. I knew this was coming because of how Saul treated me." But that wasn't David's response.

While David had suffered at the hand of Saul, there had been good things in his relationship as well. David, a simple shepherd from the backwoods, had been given the opportunity to learn the ways of ruling in the palace by living with Saul and watching him rule. Rather than focusing on the bad, David remembered the good that Saul had done, both for Israel and for him personally. As a result, Saul's death caused David, a mighty war hero, to mourn and weep.

David and Absalom—Years later, David would experience another tragic moment in his life. His son Absalom rebelled against him and was ultimately killed. One of the most moving passages in the Bible on grief describes King David's reaction to the death of Absalom.

> *And the king said unto Cushi, Is the young man Absalom safe? And Cushi answered, The enemies of my lord the king, and all that rise against thee to do thee hurt, be as that young man is. And the king was much moved, and went up to the chamber over the gate, and wept: and as he went, thus he said, O my son Absalom, my son, my son Absalom! would God I had died for thee, O Absalom, my son, my son!*
> —2 SAMUEL 18:32–33

When David heard that Absalom had lost his life, his heart was broken. Even though Absalom had rebelled against him and driven him from Jerusalem, David would have traded his own life for his son's life.

Grief is universal—from man's fall to David's time to present day. In a sense, it's comforting to know that other people can relate to our grief, but what does grief look like in our life? How does it manifest itself?

What Grief Looks Like in Our Lives

Everyone grieves differently. But in the many studies done, doctors and psychiatrists have identified several emotions and thoughts commonly experienced in grief.

Elisabeth Kubler-Ross wrote a book called *On Death and Dying* in 1969. In her book, she described five stages of the grieving process based on her experience with the terminally ill. I've found that her observations about these five stages are helpful in processing my own emotions and understanding the emotions of others. These steps aren't necessarily universal or always sequential, but they do provide a helpful way to understand and work through the process of grief.

Denial—When you first get bad news, your world turns upside down, and you process many different emotions. But when the initial shock of the bad news wears off, the trial you're in the middle of doesn't feel real to you. Whether consciously or not, you're denying what has happened.

Anger—At some point, reality hits, and slowly, feelings of anger and unfairness build. In a sense, this feeling of unfairness is right. Many unjust and painful things do happen because we live in a sinful world.

Bargaining—Instead of praying to God for strength and comfort, the grieving person tries to bargain with Him for a change of circumstances. They might say something like, "God, if you will just help me out here, then I will_____."

Depression—Eventually, most people will realize they cannot bargain their way out of their situation, and depression sets in. No longer angry, they allow the reality of the situation to fully sink in, and in weariness and desperation, they become depressed. Instead of trying to find a way out, they give up.

Acceptance—The grieving process encompasses thousands of different, very real emotions. When we get to the point, however, when we accept the trial as something that God has allowed and will help us deal with, we're ready to begin the healing process.

Grief is a complex subject. Not only does it remind us that we live in a fallen world, but experiencing grief also reveals unique aspects of the complex and intricate way that God made *us*.

What Grief Reveals about Us

Grief is an inward emotion that every person will outwardly express differently. The Bible words used for *grief* mean "to sorrow, to suffer loss, to feel pain, to bewail, or to be angry." As we've seen with biblical examples, it's not wrong to grieve. When something bad happens, God created us with this capacity to grieve. Furthermore, grief shows three things about us.

Grief reveals our love for someone. When we hear of a soldier being killed for our nation, we hurt. We recognize the massive sacrifice they have made on our behalf. At the same time, we don't necessarily grieve. It bothers us, but it doesn't necessarily affect our day-to-day life the way true grief does. But if someone we knew personally was killed in war, we would grieve.

There is a man in our church who served our country in Iraq. I remember praying for him every day and trying to be a blessing to his wife and children in any way that I could. If he had lost his life in service, I would have grieved deeply.

Love is one of the greatest motivating factors behind our grief. Remember the story of Lazarus? Before Jesus raised Lazarus from the dead, Jesus wept. When others then saw Jesus weeping over Lazarus' death, they said "...Behold how he *loved* him!" (John 11:36). Jesus' outward expression of grief was a demonstration of His love for His friend.

Grief reveals the significance of someone to us. When we lose someone we love, we become keenly aware of their absence, and we realize their value to us and the ways they enriched our lives like never before. Sometimes we feel regret for not expressing our love or appreciation more, and we grieve when we consider our future without them.

I remember when a dear man in our church lost his wife. When I got the news and went to see him, he was composed, yet there was deep grief evident on his face. They had been married for nearly fifty-eight years.

He told me, "I don't want her to be gone. I just miss her. I wish I still had her—I didn't want it to be like this."

I asked, "What did you want?"

He replied, "I just wanted us to keep on going. I told her we had to go for seventy-five—you know, get on Paul Harvey maybe." His pain showed the depth of the loss he had suffered.

When we grieve, we reveal that we miss someone and acutely feel their loss in our lives.

Grief reveals that we have a soul. When God created us, He gave us a soul: "And the LORD God formed man of the dust of the ground, and breathed into his nostrils the breath of life; and man became a living soul" (Genesis 2:7).

When we talk about salvation, we'll sometimes say that God "saved our soul." Repeatedly, the Bible stresses the importance of our soul. Jesus Himself said, "For what shall it profit a man, if he shall gain the whole world, and lose his own soul?" (Mark 8:36).

Our soul is who we are. It is what processes and feels emotions. Our grief reveals the emotional depth with which God made us. He created us to love and feel and know one another. This means that when we lose someone or something we value, we will experience a sense of loss in these deep places of our souls.

Thankfully, God also created us with the capacity to *heal* in the deep places of our souls as well. Healing doesn't restore the loss, but it does allow us to continue in spite of it. And through the power of grace, it allows us to experience God's promises in a way we never would have known.

Healing Through Grief

When pain enters our lives, it is right and appropriate to grieve. Ecclesiastes 3:1–4 says, "To every thing there is a season, and a time to every purpose under the heaven: A time to be born, and a time to die; a time to plant, and a time to pluck up that which is planted; A time to kill, and a time to heal; a time to break down, and a time to build up; A time to weep, and a time to laugh; a time to mourn, and a time to dance."

Yes, there is a time to laugh, but the Bible designates a time to mourn as well. David, who understood what it was like to suffer, wrote, "Thou tellest my wanderings: put thou my tears into thy bottle: are they not in thy book?" (Psalm 56:8). In this verse, David was referring to a tiny jar called a lachrymatory. Usually made of clay, it was used to collect the tears of mourning loved ones as an expression of their sadness. Sometimes they would bury that jar of tears with or near their loved one or place it upon their grave. They thought their evidences of grief were significant enough to be kept as a remembrance.

In fact, such tear bottles were still used into Victorian times. The tears for a dead loved one would be captured in a bottle, and when the tears had evaporated, the official mourning period would be considered over.

The entire Psalm in which this verse is found is a song David wrote when he was hiding from Saul among the Philistines in Gath. Certainly he had much to mourn over in those days. In effect, David said, "I am weeping and crying, but *I* am not collecting the tears. Will *You* please collect them for me?" We might say, "God, please notice that I'm hurting."

Grieving is both appropriate, expected, and a necessary part of the healing process.

In fact, the prophet Ezekiel's story shows us that it is an anomaly for someone *not* to grieve. God had Ezekiel do many strange things as signs to the nation of Israel, but one of the more remarkable ones involved his wife. Ezekiel loved his wife dearly. In fact, the Bible says that she was "the desire of his eyes." Yet, after her sudden death, God told him not to mourn for her.

> *Son of man, behold, I take away from thee the desire of thine eyes with a stroke: yet neither shalt thou mourn nor weep, neither shall thy tears run down. Forbear to cry, make no mourning for the dead, bind the tire of thine head upon thee, and put on thy shoes upon thy feet, and cover not thy lips, and eat not the bread of men. So I spake unto the people in the morning: and at even my wife died; and I did in the morning as I was commanded.*
> —EZEKIEL 24:16–18

Ezekiel obeyed God's command and did not grieve for his beloved wife. God doesn't have to command someone to grieve; it is so normal *to* grieve that He had to command Ezekiel *not* to grieve. God knew that Ezekiel's unnatural reaction would attract the Israelites' attention and that they would question his unusual behavior (Ezekiel 24:19), allowing Ezekiel to convey God's message to this captive audience.

So why does God allow us to grieve in the first place? Wouldn't it be easier if He would simply erase our pain? God created us as emotional beings, and the same heart that feels love will feel loss. I believe grieving is the outlet God gives us for expressing such intense emotions. You might grieve very differently than the way I would grieve. Some people express grief with great outward emotion. Others are quieter with how they grieve and may only show it in their private moments.

When we express what we feel, it helps us to process our emotions. And we shouldn't be afraid or ashamed of expressing them because we think it makes us look weak or unspiritual. Consider the Bible characters we've already talked about—Jacob, Job, and David. All of them freely expressed their emotions. Grieving is part of the process that helps us to heal.

On the side of the tires on my car is a warning against over-inflating. If I fill my tires with too much air, they will eventually explode. A buildup of excess pressure is dangerous—not only to tires, but to people. Grieving does not rid us of sorrow, but it does help release some of the pressure.

Harmful or Helpful?

It comes down to a choice. When we walk through a trial, we can choose a harmful or helpful response to grief. The right response to grief is to draw closer to the Lord. We'll have a more tender heart, a more open spirit, and a greater willingness to help those around us.

But the wrong response is to allow grief to make us bitter. Instead of turning toward God, we turn away from Him in anger. Remember Naomi from the book of Ruth? She, along with her husband and two sons, went to Moab because of a famine in Israel. If you study her story, you'll see that her and her husband's decision reveals a lack of faith and confidence in God.

Eventually, Naomi's sons met and married girls from Moab. Sometime later, tragedy struck. Both her sons and her husband died, and Naomi found herself a widow in a strange country.

Ultimately, Naomi decided to return to Bethlehem, but urged her daughters-in-law to remain behind. Orpah agreed, but Ruth refused and insisted on accompanying Naomi back to Israel. In the following passage, we see Naomi's response to the people when she returned. Can you see in it how her bitterness twisted her perspective?

> And she said unto them, Call me not Naomi, call me Mara: for the Almighty hath dealt very bitterly with me. I went out full and the LORD hath brought me home again empty: why then call ye me Naomi, seeing the LORD hath testified against me, and the Almighty hath afflicted me?—RUTH 1:20–21

Naomi said she went to Moab because she was full. The truth was she left because of a famine. She said that she came back empty, but she was accompanied by the loyal and loving Ruth. Later in the story, Naomi did turn back to the Lord. But this first response to grief was the wrong response.

Naomi's actions are a lesson to us. When you are grieving, your mind can twist things into being much worse than they actually are. Even when reality is unimaginably difficult, we can make it even worse by refusing to remember the blessings God has given us.

Naomi's response to grief was bitterness. Now, let's fast-forward four generations to David. His wrong response to grief resulted in wrong actions. In 1 Samuel, we find David at Ziklag. This was a low point in David's life. In the middle of running from Saul, he joined the Philistines.

While there, he lied to Achish, the king of Gath. He said he was fighting the Israelites (1 Samuel 27:10) while instead fighting the common enemies of the Philistines and the Israelites. He only wanted Achish to think that he was totally against Israel and on the side of this Philistine king. But David took his deception a step further and killed everybody he fought—including the women "Lest... they should tell on us..." (1 Samuel 27:11)—just to preserve this lie.

David should have trusted God and realized that because he was God's choice to rule Israel, there was no chance that Saul could kill him. He should have said something like, "Saul can hunt me with 3,000 men or with

300,000 men; he can throw three javelins at me or thirty javelins at me. God said I am going to be the next king of Israel, and that cannot happen if I am dead."

Instead of trusting God for his safety, David tried to solve his problem on his own by running away. As a result, he lied and killed innocent people. Ultimately, that deception would have horrific ramifications. Because David failed to obey the Lord, he brought upon himself a time of grief.

One day, when David and his men went off to battle, they returned to find their wives and children gone and the entire city burned to the ground. The Bible says the men wept until they had no more power to weep. As a result of their anger over what they had lost, the men began to discuss stoning David (1 Samuel 30:6).

They basically decided, "We wouldn't be in this mess if we hadn't followed David. We had a decent home where we lived before. We followed this guy thinking that he was something special. He led us to believe there was some great plan for the future, and now look at the mess he's gotten us into."

This was a wrong response by the men as well. Their grief caused them to grow angry at their God-ordained leader. How do we respond when we're in a situation like the one David and his men were in? Do we find fellowship and comfort in our church family? Do we look to godly mentors for help in the grieving process? Or do we turn our back on the Lord? The devil might whisper in our ear: *Look, you've been doing right, you've been faithful to church, you read your Bible every day, you've given to the building fund, you're involved in ministry…and look how God treated you. You should just give up. Why bother serving a God that can't even prevent trials from happening in your life?*

We succumb to Satan's lies, and like David's men, begin contemplating things we never would have considered before. David's men began to plot his death.

In God's mercy, He ultimately worked the situation for good, and the women and children were safely returned. But the point remains—grief changes us.

In 1 Chronicles 4:9–10, we come to a fascinating phrase in a prayer by Jabez. He prayed for productivity and God's power, but he finally asked for protection from evil "that it may not grieve me!" Jabez realized that in the middle of blessing, spiritual increase, and enjoyment of the power of God in his life, he could still fall into sin. Jabez knew that sin's consequences often cause grief.

God's Promises for Grief

Over the past few pages, you may have noticed a recurring theme. Whether or not we come out from a trial stronger than we were before hinges on our response to grief.

Foundational to everything else we're going to discuss, realize that God wants to comfort you. God is not an angry, impersonal being that doesn't care when His children suffer. On the contrary, He delights in comforting His children. Jesus said, "Blessed are they that mourn: for they shall be comforted" (Matthew 5:4).

This is an amazing promise. The God of all comfort (2 Corinthians 1:3) wants to help those who mourn. Family and friends can offer comfort, but they are fallible humans. God, however, never changes. He won't let you down. He is always there to provide solace and comfort.

When you're in the valley, you get to know the Saviour in a deeper way than you would on the mountaintop. Run to the Lord when you're walking through a hard time. You'll experience a sweetness that rarely comes in a time of victory and success. Ask Him for help when you're hurting. He created you, knows you, and loves you more than anyone ever could. When you rest in Him, you will experience His comfort.

Also foundational to dealing with grief is seeking out others who have gone through a similar difficulty. Grief often forges close bonds between you and another person who has experienced the same trial that you have. Others have experienced betrayal by someone they thought they could trust, have lost a loved one, or have experienced great financial difficulty. Sometimes, recognizing that others have experienced what you're going through now makes grief easier to bear. We're encouraged knowing that if others can make it through grief, we can too.

Jesus said, "Blessed are ye, when men shall revile you, and persecute you, and shall say all manner of evil against you falsely, for my sake. Rejoice, and be exceeding glad: for great is your reward in heaven: for so persecuted they the prophets which were before you" (Matthew 5:11–12).

This passage reminds me of Hebrews 11, the great faith chapter of the Bible. Sometimes, we refer to this as God's Hall of Faith. We read about Moses, Abraham, Enoch, Abel, Joshua, and Rahab. All of these heroes of the faith endured hardship and difficulty. I believe one of the reasons that God tells us their stories is to remind us that others have gone through the same troubles that we're going through.

Remember others who have suffered. If people persecute you for your faith, you're in good company—Peter and Paul were too. If others reject you, you're not alone—Jesus was too. It's an incredible comfort to know that no matter what we face, there are others who have experienced the same type of pain and made it to the other side.

The final foundational aspect to dealing with grief is accepting it. Jeremiah 10:19 says, "Woe is me for my hurt! my wound is grievous; but I said, Truly this is a grief, and I must bear it." Today, he might have said, "I don't like grief; I can't avoid it; I can't pretend it's not there, but I must bear it." This isn't easy to do or say. Ultimately, however, we have to recognize that grief is a universal reality of our fallen world, and we must accept the trial we are going through.

A wonderful promise comes when we accept trials. Look at 2 Corinthians 12:9–10:

> *And he said unto me, My grace is sufficient for thee: for my strength is made perfect in weakness. Most gladly therefore will I rather glory in my infirmities, that the power of Christ may rest upon me. Therefore I take pleasure in infirmities, in reproaches, in necessities, in persecutions, in distresses for Christ's sake: for when I am weak, then am I strong.*—2 CORINTHIANS 12:9–10

Paul is talking here about his thorn in the flesh. He begged God three times to remove it from him, but God told him no. He wanted Paul to learn to rely on His strength and grace. Like Paul, we don't need to like all the things that God brings into our lives, but we do have to accept them. And the only way we can do this is through the grace of God.

I'm thankful that, while we are to accept grief, we don't have to deal with it alone. Look what David wrote in Psalm 18.

> *I will call upon the LORD, who is worthy to be praised: so shall I be saved from mine enemies. In my distress I called upon*

the LORD, and cried unto my God: he heard my voice out of his temple, and my cry came before him, even into his ears.
—PSALM 18:3, 6

This is a Psalm that David wrote to celebrate God's delivering him from King Saul. David was in great danger, but instead of complaining, he called on the Lord. When you're in trouble or going through a time of grief, don't run *from* God; run *to* God. Don't drift away from God; get closer to God. When you feel you're going under, hold tighter to His hand. God makes a place of protection for us as His children, and He invites us to ask for His help when we are hurting and in need.

Years ago, I saw a painting that showed a raging fire in the forest and a group of animals running toward an ark. The title of the painting was "Refuge." Like the ark in the picture, God is a refuge. He is always faithful—run to Him and seek His help. He stands ready to give you comfort for every grief you're given.

"Trust in him at all times; ye people, pour out your heart before him: God is a refuge for us. Selah" (Psalm 62:8).

TWO

RESISTING TEMPTATION

One of the largest freshwater turtles is the alligator snapping turtle. Found primarily in the southeastern United States, these massive turtles have been known to weigh close to 250 pounds. They are carnivorous, and while their diet is primarily fish, they have been known to eat almost anything else they can find in the water—sometimes even small alligators.

The alligator snapping turtle relies on a uniquely deceitful method of hunting for fish. The turtle will lie completely still on the floor of a lake or river with its mouth open wide. At the end of its tongue is a small, pink, worm-shaped appendage. The turtle wiggles its tongue so that it looks like a worm moving through the water. When a fish comes to eat the worm, the turtle's jaws rapidly close, trapping the fish.[1]

Just as the snapping turtle knows how to lure unsuspecting prey to its death, Satan knows exactly how to tempt us to sin. The Bible says that Satan "…as a roaring lion, walketh about, seeking whom he may devour" (1 Peter 5:8). Temptation always comes in the guise of something desirable, but its end result is destruction.

This is why it is important that we know *beforehand* how we are going to respond to temptation. The wrong time to establish convictions is when we're in the middle of a temptation. During that time, the heart is strongly pulled toward sin. While it's not impossible to remain strong in the middle of temptation, it is much more difficult if you're not prepared for the temptation.

How then do we establish safeguards in our heart against temptation? How do we avoid becoming the devil's next victim? When we're under that moment of pressure, how do we stand firm?

If anyone could relate to the pressure temptation brings into our lives, it would be Joseph. In his example, we see several key principles for victory over Satan's temptations, which encourage us that we too can emerge victorious over temptation.

---

[1] "The Deceitfulness of Sin," *Ministry127.com,* http://ministry127.com/resources/illustration/the-deceitfulness-of-sin (accessed October 17, 2018).

A Searing Betrayal

To say that Joseph walked through a difficult time would be an understatement. Jacob, Joseph's father, doted on him, and Joseph's brothers grew jealous of their father's obvious favoritism. To make matters worse, Jacob gave Joseph a coat of many colors—a symbol of the fact that Joseph did not do the type of manual labor that his brothers did. On top of that, Joseph revealed the strange dreams he had been having—dreams of one day ruling over his brothers.

Joseph's brothers were now angry with him. Instead of rejoicing over his success, they began to plot his demise. One day, Joseph traveled to watch his brothers work and to report their progress to Jacob. When he realized they were failing in their responsibilities, Joseph gave the negative report to Jacob. Finally, the brothers had had enough. The next time he came to check on them, as they saw him coming, they decided to kill him. They took him, stripped him of the hated coat of many colors, and put him in a pit while they sat and ate lunch.

As they ate, a caravan of Midianite slave traders came by, and the brothers changed their minds. Instead of *only* being rid of him, they decided to make a profit and sold Joseph into slavery.

Slowly, Joseph and this caravan made their way toward Egypt. When they finally arrived, Joseph found himself standing for sale in the middle of an Egyptian slave market.

Imagine how humiliating the surrounding conversation would have been as he stood next to the others being sold into slavery.

"I don't know about that one," one man might have said to his friend. "He looks a little weak. I probably couldn't get one good day of work out of him."

Another man may have commented, "Look at that one's posture. He's probably going to have back problems." How degrading this would have been in Joseph's life as he stood there, listening to people talk about how much he was worth as human merchandise.

Finally, a man named Potiphar bought Joseph. Remember—Joseph had been bought twice, first by the Midianites for their slave caravan, and then by Potiphar.

Because of the actions instigated by Joseph's brother's jealousy, Joseph went from being a revered member of his father's house to being a slave. What a drastic change—a slave has absolutely no choice over his destiny, his direction, or his decisions. Some masters were kinder and more tolerant than others. Some gave their slaves a degree of autonomy. But nothing changed the fact that they were still owned. They couldn't quit or change jobs if they didn't like what they were told to do.

Every day, Joseph woke up with the knowledge that it was his own brothers who had sold him into slavery. It would have been easy for the betrayal to make Joseph bitter. The temptation for all of us is to let trials lead us to bitterness.

Despite all that had happened to him, however, Joseph refused to lose his belief in who he was and who God was. Because of his attitude and performance, Potiphar recognized that Joseph was a diligent worker and promoted him to a position of responsibility within his household. Genesis 39:3 says, "And his master saw that the LORD was with him, and that the LORD made all that he did to prosper in his hand." Potiphar recognized that the God Joseph served was doing something in his life. He realized that whenever Joseph was over something, things went well.

As a result, Potiphar promoted Joseph. Genesis 39:4 says, "And Joseph found grace in his sight, and he served him: and he made him overseer over his house, and all that he had he put into his hand."

This is an incredible amount of power for a young man such as Joseph. Everything that Potiphar had was placed under his responsibility. Potiphar had such complete confidence in Joseph that "he knew not aught he had, save the bread which he did eat" (Genesis 39:6). Not only did Potiphar place Joseph in charge, he didn't even check up on him.

Potiphar made a wise choice in selecting Joseph, for everything Joseph did caused Potiphar to prosper. "And it came to pass from the time that he had made him overseer in his house, and over all that he had, that the LORD blessed the Egyptian's house for Joseph's sake; and the blessing of the LORD was upon all that he had in the house, and in the field" (Genesis 39:5).

I doubt that many of us would respond as well as Joseph did. In fact, I think our natural, fleshly response would be to do our work sullenly and as slowly as possible. We'd fight the injustice in our life and look for every opportunity to escape or to get back at our captors. But Joseph chose to do his best, and God blessed him immensely. He was exalted from lowly slave to leader in Potiphar's house. In this amazing transformation of circumstances, we see an important lesson about faithfulness.

Over the years, I've seen some people remain faithful to God when things grew difficult. As they struggled, worked, and prayed, He responded and blessed them. That faithfulness and effort is commendable. But when things began to look up, these same people began to turn away from the Lord. All of a sudden, church wasn't as important as it used to be. Tithing gave way to saving for a beach house. Because of their good fortune, they fell into the mindset of thinking things were going well because they were somehow special. This way of thinking is dangerous. Our circumstances will change, but our faithfulness and commitment to the Lord should not. Joseph is a great example of this. He was faithful to the Lord as he stood in a slave market, but he was also faithful when he was promoted to a high position in Potiphar's house.

Soon, however, a time of extreme temptation would enter his life.

In the Face of Temptation

Everything seemed to be looking up for Joseph. Many Bible scholars believe Joseph was only about eighteen years old, but he had already risen to a position of power and influence. Joseph was probably looking forward to a good future. But then temptation came.

Genesis 39:7 summarizes: "And it came to pass after these things, that his master's wife cast her eyes upon Joseph; and she said, Lie with me."

History tells us that the actions of Potiphar's wife were the norm. In Egypt's promiscuous society, an owner would often take a slave and force that slave into an immoral relationship. There's no indication that Potiphar's wife expected Joseph to refuse her. She didn't ask if Joseph was interested; she didn't flirt with him; she just bluntly commanded him. It's likely that she had indulged herself in that kind of relationship before without any consequences and expected this time to be the same.

Joseph was an attractive man. Genesis 39:6 says, "…And Joseph was a goodly person, and well favoured." No wonder Potiphar's wife noticed her husband's handsome, well-built slave.

The devil likes to twist the gifts God has given you. God had blessed Joseph physically, but the devil used it to get Potiphar's wife to tempt him to sin. But what about your life? If God has blessed you with extraordinary talents, you can be tempted to laziness. If you have a charismatic personality, the devil may tempt you to take advantage of others. If you're blessed with intelligence, the devil can tempt you to be proud. God has given each of us gifts to use for Him, and we should develop them. But we also need to be aware that the devil will use them against us to tempt us.

If we were in Joseph's position, it's likely that we would be somewhat flattered by Potiphar's wife's proposition. Flattery is an effective tool the devil uses. But don't succumb to his advances. As God's children, we have certain rights and privileges, and one of those is strength to overcome any temptation.

Let's look at Joseph's response to Potiphar's wife. He didn't stop to think the answer over. He didn't leave room for her to ask again later. He didn't say, "That might not be the greatest idea, but I'll think about it."

He firmly said, "No."

Responding immediately when you are tempted is crucial. The longer we wait to do right, the harder it gets.

Joseph left no room for doubt—the Bible simply says he refused.

Franklin P. Jones, an American journalist in the 1900s, said, "What makes resisting temptation difficult for many people is that they don't want to discourage it completely." Not responding promptly to the Holy Spirit's leading places you at risk.

Years ago, my father and I were in a bowling alley and began discussing someone who was going through a difficult time. When I told my father that this man and his family were really having financial issues, he immediately reached into his wallet and pulled out a $50 bill. He insisted, "Give this to them."

At the time, my dad was between churches, and I knew that he didn't have much himself. I suggested he wait. He said, "No. I learned a long time ago that if I don't respond to generous impulses immediately, I'll talk myself out of doing what I ought to do."

Whether the Holy Spirit prompts us to do something we might not otherwise have done (such as He did to my father) or to resist an impulse to which we might have otherwise succumbed (such as a temptation), we should respond immediately.

Refusing temptation once, however, doesn't mean it will immediately go away. Satan will not give up just because you say no once. The devil will keep tempting you again and again, trying to see if he can catch you with your armor off and your guard down. He is patient. If he doesn't get you the first time, he'll come back. Even after Jesus refused Satan's temptations, Satan only left for a little while. Luke 4:13 says, "And when the devil had ended all the temptation, he departed from him for a season."

One reason why Joseph's story is such a good example of how we should respond to temptation is that it so clearly illustrates this tactic of our enemy. Satan knows that over time, we become accustomed to sin and it no longer repels us as it did when we were first exposed to it. This is true even if we continue to resist the temptation. Alexander Pope wrote about this in his famous *Essay on Man*.

> Vice is a monster of so frightful mien,
> As to be hated needs but to be seen;
> Yet seen too oft, familiar with her face,
> We first endure, then pity, then embrace.
> —Alexander Pope

Sin, if we're not careful, will slowly become more and more attractive to us. Potiphar's wife was persistent in her pursuit of Joseph. Genesis 39:10 says, "And it came to pass, as she spake to Joseph day by day, that he hearkened not unto her, to lie by her, or to be with her." Instead of giving up when Joseph repeatedly turned her down, she was determined to get what she wanted.

Joseph chose not to entertain the idea of sinning with Potiphar's wife, but she was persistent. Had Joseph not taken the temptation seriously, his life could have turned out entirely differently. Likewise, when we don't take the danger of temptation seriously, destructive things can occur.

The final eruption of Mount St. Helens in May of 1980 was not a sudden event. For two months prior to the massive blast—the most deadly and destructive in American history—earthquakes and volcanic activity signaled a major event was underway. Authorities had plenty of time to sound the alarm and warn those living nearby of the looming danger. Yet despite the seriousness of the threat, some people chose to disregard the warnings.

Probably the best known of those who refused to evacuate was Harry Randall Truman. The eighty-three year old man was the owner and caretaker at the Mount St. Helens Lodge at Spirit Lake. He had survived the sinking of his troop ship by a German submarine off the coast of Ireland during World War I, and he was not about to leave just because scientists thought there was danger. Truman told reporters, "I don't have any idea whether it will blow. But I don't believe it to the point that I'm going to pack up." On May 18, 1980, Truman and his lodge were buried beneath 150 feet of mud and debris from the volcanic eruption. His body was never found.[2]

---

[2] Dick Thompson, *Volcano Cowboys* (New York, New York: St. Martin's Press, 2000), quoted in "Get Out!" *Ministry127.com,* http://ministry127. com/resources/illustration/get-out (accessed October 17, 2018).

We shake our heads at this story. How could someone just ignore such obvious danger? It is foolish to recognize danger or temptation and think that we will somehow be exempt from the consequences if we linger. If we believe Scripture's warnings concerning temptation, we will surely flee. In fact, when you think you are strong, you are at even greater risk. Paul wrote, "Now all these things happened unto them for ensamples: and they are written for our admonition, upon whom the ends of the world are come. Wherefore let him that thinketh he standeth take heed lest he fall" (1 Corinthians 10:11–12).

Joseph was careful in guarding himself against the opportunity for Potiphar's wife to tempt him, even making arrangements as much as possible so he would not be exposed to the temptation she was offering him. Genesis 39:10 says "... as she spake to Joseph day by day, that he hearkened not unto her, to lie by her, *or to be with her.*"

This is important. If you know something tempts you to sin, get rid of it. If you know a program on television is bad, stop watching it. If you have a radio station that plays worldly music, change the button on the radio. Temptations will not just go away by themselves. We have to take precautions to avoid the temptation. Romans 13:14 says, "But put ye on the Lord Jesus Christ, and make not provision for the flesh, to fulfil the lusts thereof."

Fleeing Temptation's Clutches

Genesis 39:12 shows the climax of Joseph's temptation. Potiphar's wife literally grabbed Joseph by the garment and asked him to sleep with her. Joseph, just as he had done before, adamantly refused. In fact, the Bible says he "…left his garment in her hand, and fled, and got him out" (Genesis 39:12).

Did you catch how this verse says that a) he fled, and b) he got out? Immediately, a picture is painted in our minds that Joseph fled as quickly as possible. Instead of remaining in her presence, he severed all ties with her.

We need to take that same firm stance against sin as Joseph did. If something tempts us, sometimes the greatest thing we can do is not to just hope that we'll be able to stand firm against the temptation, but to entirely cut the temptation off.

Jesus said, "And if thy right eye offend thee, pluck it out, and cast it from thee…" (Matthew 5:29). Here, Jesus used hyperbole to emphasize the importance of avoiding sin. He didn't just say, "Wear sunglasses!" He said, "Pluck out your eye."

Proverbs 22:3 says, "A prudent man foreseeth the evil, and hideth himself: but the simple pass on, and are punished." If you see temptation lurking around the corner, flee it.

This is one of the key messages throughout 1 and 2 Timothy. Paul is warning Timothy to flee temptation. In 2 Timothy 2:22 he says, "Flee also youthful lusts: but follow righteousness, faith, charity, peace, with them that call on the Lord out of a pure heart." Like Timothy and Joseph, this is vitally important for each of us to follow.

Joseph's commitment to doing right did not come without its consequences, however. When Joseph flatly refused Potiphar's wife, she, perhaps angry and humiliated, had him thrown into prison.

But God was faithful. He used Joseph's circumstances to elevate him to a position he needed to fill. Eventually, Joseph would become the second-most powerful ruler in Egypt.

At this point, you may be thinking, "I get it. I know I'm supposed to flee temptation. But how?" A quick look at three principles from Joseph's life begins to reveal the answer.

Joseph remembered the privilege he had. In the early stages of Potiphar's wife's pursuit, Joseph had refused, saying, "…Behold, my master wotteth not what is with me in the house, and he hath committed all that he hath to my hand" (Genesis 39:8). Potiphar had placed enormous trust and responsibility in Joseph. Joseph had been given a privilege that was accorded to very few slaves.

Likewise, it is a privilege to be a child and servant of God. Nothing we do can ever separate us from Jesus

Christ; we are completely secure in Him. Furthermore, God promises to forgive us when we ask Him to. Yet we should never take the promise of forgiveness of sin as an excuse to do whatever we want. Our love for Christ should motivate us to *follow* the Lord in whatever He desires, not to turn away from him.

Someone once told Charles Spurgeon, "If I believed what you believe about eternal security, I'd sin all I wanted!"

Spurgeon replied, "I sin much more than I want."

Spurgeon's response was the one that we too should have. God has saved us and placed us into His family. Romans 6:11 explains that we do not have to yield to temptation: "Likewise reckon ye also yourselves to be dead indeed unto sin, but alive unto God through Jesus Christ our Lord."

Our old man—our sin nature from birth—is constantly fighting to get us to fall into sin. But remember, you're not a slave to sin. You're a child of God! With the Lord's help, you can reckon yourself to be dead to sin and defeat temptation.

Joseph remembered who he was. Joseph told Potiphar's wife, "There is none greater in this house than I" (Genesis 39:9). Because of his position of responsibility and prominence, there were things he could not do because of the job that he held.

A police officer once told me about another officer who went to the gas pump at the station intended for filling up the squad cars. He pumped $13.00 worth of gas into his personal car and didn't pay for it. He didn't know, however, that the transaction was caught on videotape. He lost his job, his pension, his years of service, and his testimony, all for a measly $13.00.

When the thought came to him to take advantage of his privilege for personal gain, he should have responded, "I'm a policeman. I can't steal. I'm in charge of keeping others from stealing. The station warns people that, if they drive off without paying for the gas they pumped, someone like me will arrest them. I have to do what is right because of my position." Because he did not focus on his position as a reason for right behavior, he lost that position.

Joseph said, "Neither hath he kept back any thing from me but thee, because thou art his wife…" (Genesis 39:9). Potiphar's wife didn't belong to Joseph; she belonged to her husband. Joseph realized that taking her for his own, even if she wanted him to do so, would violate the principle of ownership.

When we have the chance to do something that scripturally is off-limits, it shouldn't be on our radar to even consider violating the principles of God's Word. It ought to be unthinkable to us.

Satan tries to make sin look exciting, intriguing, and even reasonable. Years ago, I took a trip to preach in New York. I flew out early and wanted to spend time sightseeing. While I was downtown, I saw a couple of disheveled men sitting on the sidewalk. They had a little cardboard box set up with three cards on it. They would move the cards around and ask people to guess which card was the red one. After watching them for a little while, I realized that the red card had a mark on it. I had thirty dollars with me and thought, *I could double my money by playing their game.*

I had one of those conversations with myself. *It's not right to gamble. But it's not gambling—I know which card the red one is!* I genuinely thought about it (briefly), but I knew it was wrong and walked away. I went into a drugstore and talked to the man at the counter. "You could make a lot of money at that game," I said.

He just smiled. "You'd win once," he said. "And then you'd lose everything you had." He explained to me that they have another marked card that looks like the red one but is black. They use it after they get you into the game.

The reason I didn't gamble was not because I was afraid to lose. In fact, I was wrongly convinced that I would win. The reason I didn't gamble was because I recognized the principle and wasn't willing to violate it, even for something that looked like a sure thing.

As we've mentioned before, Joseph said, "…How then can I do this great wickedness, and sin against God?" (Genesis 39:9). If you just look at sin as being between you and other people, it's easy to rationalize wrongdoing. But if you look at things as being between you and God, rationalizing becomes much more difficult.

Joseph refused temptation because he did not want to sin against God. Other considerations influenced Joseph, but this was the one that overrode all others. Every sin is ultimately an act of defiance against God.

David said, "Against thee, thee only, have I sinned, and done this evil in thy sight: that thou mightest be justified when thou speakest, and be clear when thou judgest" (Psalm 51:4). David's sin affected many other people. But he realized that the real issue was that he had sinned against God.

When we truly recognize the magnitude of God's love and compassion for us, sin will begin to look less appealing. Christ died for us, paid for our sins, saved us, and gave us the Holy Spirit. Christ must be the one of paramount importance when we are choosing whether or not to yield to temptation.

Remember the consequences of sin. When you're tempted, also consider what the final outcome may be. Think about the wages of sin, not just the enticements of sin. What does the Bible say about the consequences of sin? Is it worth it?

Sin always follows us. I spent the summer of 1971 working on the staff of a church in Michigan. There was a sweet elderly man there who played the piano for the church. While he has long since been in Heaven, I still remember when he came to my wedding. It was at my wedding that

I got a sobering glimpse into how sin's consequences can follow us.

At the wedding, my in-laws recognized him. He had previously lived in their city and worked as an accountant. He had stolen money from his company and given all of it away to the poor. When he was found out, he was fired and moved away in disgrace. I was shocked to hear about this man's past. I'm sure he had good intentions, but the reputation from his sin had stuck to him, even years later.

It has been said that sin will always take you further than you want to go; it will always keep you longer than you want to stay; and it will always make you pay more than you want to pay. Remember sin's consequences when you are tempted. At first, sin will seem pleasurable— something that you can handle. But in the end, it always results in destruction.

Victory Is Yours

Will we face temptation in our life? Absolutely. But God promises they don't have to defeat us. First Corinthians 10:13 says, "There hath no temptation taken you but such as is common to man: but God is faithful, who will not suffer you to be tempted above that ye are able; but will with the temptation also make a way to escape, that ye may be able to bear it."

What an amazing promise! God is faithful. He will always help us remain firm against the devil's attacks. We can live for Christ, even under the pressure of the devil.

The alligator snapping turtle knows exactly how to destroy his prey. The devil is the same way. He constantly bombards us with cleverly disguised opportunities to sin. But we don't have to be the next victim. As Joseph's story powerfully reminds us, we can flee sin.

When temptation comes knocking in your life, ask the Lord for strength to stand against the devil's tactics. Joseph gives us a great example of how to defeat temptation. But even more than Joseph, we have the Holy Spirit inside us to lead us, guide us, and give us power over sin. We have God's completed Word to memorize as we ward off Satan's attacks. And we have God's promise that no temptation is too great for us, with the Lord's help, to overcome.

Victory is yours!

THREE

RESPONDING WHEN YOU LOSE YOUR LEADER

For years, the people had enjoyed the stability of a succession of strong leaders. Their first leader had led them out of horrendous captivity through the desert. He was the mouthpiece of God for the nation, giving the commands from the Lord to govern their affairs and dictate how they should live.

When this leader passed off the scene, a young, courageous man stepped up, ordained by God. He led the people into their new homeland. He helped them claim the victory over the enemy cities God had promised to them. He encouraged the people to follow God's laws. He took a bold stand against sin. Even after his death, the older men, or the elders, continued to lead the nation to love and serve God.

But then the elders died. Without godly leaders, the nation fell into sin. This is the story of Israel.

> *And the people served the LORD all the days of Joshua, and all the days of the elders that outlived Joshua, who had seen all the great works of the LORD, that he did for Israel. And Joshua the son of Nun, the servant of the LORD, died, being an hundred and ten years old. And they buried him in the border of his inheritance in Timnathheres, in the mount of Ephraim, on the north side of the hill Gaash. And also all that generation were gathered unto their fathers: and there arose another generation after them, which knew not the LORD, nor yet the works which he had done for Israel. And the children of Israel did evil in the sight of the LORD, and served Baalim: And they forsook the LORD God of their fathers, which brought them out of the land of Egypt, and followed other gods, of the gods of the people that were round about them, and bowed themselves unto them, and provoked the LORD to anger.*
> —JUDGES 2:7–12.

It did not take long for Israel to abandon her faith for idols. What was once a nation that revered the Lord now became steeped in wickedness. It generally seemed that the spiritual temperature of Israel was dependent on the spiritual temperature of the leader.

As we read Israel's story, we're left scratching our heads, wondering what happened. The moment the Israelites lost their leader, their faith began to falter. Was their faith that shallow in the first place? Were there things that they could have done to avoid the emptiness that happened after the death of Moses and then Joshua? Even more importantly, how should we respond when we lose our leader? Does Israel's path have to be ours?

Losing a leader is something all of us will encounter, and it can be a time of confusion, fear, sadness, and even anger. Those emotions are natural. But how we ultimately respond reveals where our confidence was placed. Were we relying on God, or were we relying on the leader? Where we place our confidence makes a massive difference in our response to the loss of a leader.

The Israelites learned this lesson the hard way. Throughout the book of Judges, we see a consistent cycle. Israel would sin, then God would send a nation to judge them. From their bondage, the people would cry out to God for deliverance. He would respond, and they would experience rest. But then they would turn to idolatry. And so the cycle repeated itself. They were committed to

49

following their leader, but they were never truly committed to following God.

When a leader dies, resigns, or even moves to a different position, it can be incredibly difficult to know how to respond. Times of transition are true pressure points in our lives. But when we're under that pressure, we have a choice: we can allow the transition to be a breaking point, or we can allow the pressure to mold us into being better servants for the Lord because our eyes are focused back on Christ.

In this chapter, my prayer is to help you cultivate the right response toward not just losing a leader, but taking preventative action to avoid the path of the Israelites. And if you're a leader, my goal is to share with you how to encourage those who follow you to keep their focus on the Lord.

Following the Leader

The impact a leader can have is powerful. Imagine Great Britain without Elizabeth I or Winston Churchill. Think of America without George Washington or Abraham Lincoln. The path of these nations could have been entirely different without those great leaders. A leader can persuade an entire nation with incredible speeches. He can faithfully lead soldiers to victory in a crucial battle. He can comfort his people in times of war and distress. He can lead his nation to incredible success and worldwide power. A spiritual leader, such as a pastor, can challenge and encourage those around him to serve God with their whole hearts.

Leadership is established by God and is a natural part of how we interact with others. In any group of two or more, a leader and follower will always emerge, whether or not either recognizes the title. Almost all of us are leaders to someone. It may be that you are a parent, work in a Sunday school, teach seventh grade math, pastor a church, or are a mature believer who someone in your church looks up to. Whatever your role as a leader may be, you have an important job. It's a position that can sway others to do right...or to do wrong.

For most of this chapter, we'll look at leadership through the lens of a pastor and a church. But these principles apply in any leadership setting—whether you are the leader or the follower, and especially if you are in a pressure-filled season of leadership transition.

When a leader has the hand of God on his life, people recognize that something special is going on. They want to be part of it. They appreciate that this leader has dedicated his life to teaching others to do what is right and to encouraging them to love and serve God. They are thrilled to be part of what God is doing and grow to appreciate, admire, and love this man of God. With that privilege of leadership, however, comes great responsibility. Let's look at four specific responsibilities:

Biblical leaders need a personal, abiding walk with God. Biblical leaders have a responsibility to guide others to look to Christ, and this requires that they walk with God themselves.

In 2 Chronicles 24, we see a tragic story of a leader, King Joash, who failed to do that. Joash's spiritual leader was the priest, Jehoida, and as long as Jehoida lived, Joash served God. But when Jehoida died, Joash listened to evil counselors and allowed his heart to be drawn away from God.

How could this have happened? It would seem that Joash never developed his *own* relationship with God but simply depended on Jehoida's relationship with God. When Jehoida died, Joash had no spiritual foundation. As a result, he became prey to ungodly counsel and ideas.

If you're in training to be a new leader like Joash, analyze your relationship with the Lord. Is it genuine? Have you allowed your leader's relationship with God to be your sole source of spiritual growth, or do you also have a real relationship with the Lord? Do you spend personal time with God through His Word and in prayer? Are you seeking to grow in your walk with God? To be a successful leader, it is vitally important that you have a deep, maturing walk with God.

When you do so, you won't follow the path of Joash. When someone you looked up to passes off the scene, you won't be left scrambling to pick up the pieces and figure out what comes next. You'll have an abiding relationship with the Lord that makes the transition far smoother.

Beyond being sure that your relationship with the Lord is solid, you also need to encourage those who follow you to grow in their personal walk. Certainly they are personally accountable for their actions and decisions. But there are important things that you can do to point them in that direction.

Biblical leaders attach their followers to God, not to themselves. If you're in a position of leadership, try to deflect the attention to God. A biblical leader's mentality isn't, "It's all about me." Instead, it is, "It's all about Him!" The Apostle Paul was a great leader, but he recognized that Christ should have the preeminence, writing, "And he is the head of the body, the church: who is the beginning, the firstborn from the dead; that in all things he might have the preeminence" (Colossians 1:18).

Unfortunately, some leaders haven't developed that attitude. I know one pastor who literally asked his staff, "Do you have people working on my birthday celebration yet?" I heard of another who appointed a committee to take care of his gifts at Christmas, his birthday, and his anniversary. That self-centered attitude is the opposite of what a godly leader's attitude should be.

This doesn't mean that a leader isn't worthy of honor. But if you're a leader, it's not your job to manipulate that honor into happening. Proverbs 27:2 says, "Let another man praise thee, and not thine own mouth; a stranger, and not thine own lips." God knows how to bless those who are following Him in ways bigger than they could dream of.

The main job of the leader is not to get people to love and follow *him;* it is to get them to love and follow *God.* This is an important mentality for a spiritual leader to embrace. If members of the church are depending on your relationship with the Lord and not their own, it will be easy for them to fall away from God. One day, your paths may separate either through a ministry transition or your retirement. You want to encourage them to love God more than they love you. You want to leave an impact so that when you're gone, they will serve God with their whole hearts.

Biblical leaders should talk more about God than about themselves. As a leader, you should constantly talk about the Lord, not yourself. Even as you use personal illustrations in preaching or teaching, their purpose should not be to get people to think, *Wow, what a great leader we have.* They should be intended, planned, and presented so that people more deeply understand and immerse in the truth you are teaching. If they think anything about greatness, it should be, *Wow, what a great Lord we have.* All these things go back to the goal of pointing people to Christ.

Biblical leaders must teach commitment to principle rather than to places or people. Paul wrote, "Be ye followers of me, *even as I also am of Christ*" (1 Corinthians 11:1). The last part of this verse is key. Paul was not trying to get people to go blindly with him wherever he went; he was trying to get people to go with him as he went after Christ. When you as a leader take even one step away from God, the people following you will either continue following you down a wrong path or be forced to take a step away from you.

There have been times when I've had to step away from people I admired and respected because they were no longer closely following the Lord. That's not something I have wanted to do; it's never a comfortable position to be in. But when others have asked me to do things that I could not do and remain true to the Bible, I have had to make the decision to distance myself from those people.

Some years ago, a preacher was telling me about another pastor who made his own decisions based on the Word of God rather than on political influence.

"He's a maverick—kind of like you," he said.

I don't mind being called a maverick. I would rather be known as someone who stands alone for right than someone who goes along with what is popular. Those who follow you should never feel such an unhealthy dependence that they would trustingly follow you if you stopped following God's Word.

A Portrait of a Biblical Follower

Biblical followers recognize several key principles to ensure that their relationship with their leader is secondary to their relationship with the Lord.

Biblical followers know God; they don't just know about Him. There is danger in followers becoming so attached to the leader that they substitute the leader's relationship with God for their own. By this, I mean that instead of truly knowing God, they only know *about* what God has done through the life of the leader. They know what the leader has said about God, but they don't have a deep, personal knowledge of and relationship with Him.

For example, you know who the President of the United States is. You probably know who his family is and what his basic beliefs are. You have a general idea of what he is like. But you most likely don't know *him*. You don't share deep, personal conversations with him.

Never let that kind of relationship be similar to your relationship with God. It's not enough to just know about the miracles, to memorize verses, or to understand God's attributes. You have to know God personally and have a real, vibrant walk with Him.

Unless you are personally studying your Bible, you won't know if your leader is following God. Our desire should never be to catch our leaders doing wrong, but we also shouldn't have the mentality of blindly accepting everything the leader says. As you spend time growing in the Lord, you'll begin to develop convictions for yourself that will help you to determine what is truth and error.

Be like the Bereans. They were described as "more noble" because they went to the Word of God to determine if what Paul was teaching was correct (Acts 17:11). The Bible must be the standard against which all things are measured.

Biblical followers experience God at work in their lives; they don't just hear about it. On Sunday nights at our church, we try to have a time of testimony. I want to provide an opportunity for people to share how God is working in their lives. One of the reasons for that is to allow our young people to see what God is doing today rather than just hear about what used to happen in the past. I want God's power to seem vibrant and real and *present*.

Ask the Lord to work in your life in a way that you'll know, *Wow. That was a God moment!* An amazing spiritual refreshment comes when you see God working through you. You need to have answered prayers and truths from Scripture that you have found for yourself. I remember when my father would take me with him when he went soulwinning. Watching people pray to accept Christ as Saviour made me believe that it was possible. No one had to convince me that God could save people—I saw it happen time and time again.

In Jeremiah 33:3, God invites, "Call unto me, and I will answer thee, and show thee great and mighty things, which thou knowest not." God is a personal God. He delights in working in your life. He wants to do things that will amaze you and encourage you to draw even closer to such an incredible God.

Biblical followers rely on the Lord, not on the leader, for strength and wisdom. Years ago, a pastor in the same state where I pastor went through a couple of church splits and was having a hard time. He was a good man, and he was trying to get the people to follow the Lord, but some of them did not want to go along. He would sometimes call me for advice, and I tried to help him.

One night, this pastor's church held a vote that went against him. When his friend asked the pastor what he was going to do, he replied, "I don't know. I haven't talked to Brother Ouellette yet."

I think he said that tongue-in-cheek, but it made me uncomfortable when I heard it. Although it is wise and biblical to get counsel, no human can be the source of wisdom and direction for another. We must seek God for ourselves rather than relying on someone else.

This goes back to the biblical doctrine of the priesthood of the believer. We who have trusted Christ as our Saviour have direct access to God. We don't have to go through a priest or mediator because Christ *is* our mediator. "For there is one God, and one mediator between God and men, the man Christ Jesus" (1 Timothy 2:5).

This means that we are supposed to go to God directly for ourselves. People are *helpful*, but only God is *necessary*. People can advise us, but only God can infallibly direct us. If you stand only on what a leader counsels you to do but don't seek God for wisdom, you'll lose your way when that leader is gone. The best leader-follower relationship comes when both people are following God with their whole hearts.

Our Ultimate Leader

No matter if we're a follower or a leader, Jesus Christ *must* be our highest authority. He is our greatest leader and the one we ultimately answer to. And the amazing, comforting reality is that our God will never grow weary and quit. He will never transition to a different ministry. Even the greatest, most godly leaders we will ever know fall short of God's greatness and glory. But God is eternal. No matter what transitions come into our lives, God is always constant.

God ordained the leader/follower relationship. As long as leaders are following and loving the Lord, we should look up to godly leaders and follow them as they follow Christ. But if they choose to walk away from Christ or their authority contradicts the authority of Scripture, we must respectfully disagree with them. If we choose to abandon the Word of God for a leader, we're on unsteady ground.

Losing a leader is definitely a season of pressure. But if we place our confidence in God, not man, it won't derail our walk with the Lord. We won't suddenly falter in our relationship with God.

Know the Bible and know the God of the Bible yourself. Even if a leader is following Christ, but we choose to exalt that leader over our relationship with the Lord, we're setting ourselves up for failure. It's important to love the leader, but we should also *worship* God. Otherwise, when that leader passes off the scene, we'll be left with a void we should have been allowing Christ to fill. But if we have that strong foundation of personally knowing God, we'll remain rooted in our faith.

PART TWO

FAMILY PRESSURES

FOUR

PREPARING FOR SUCCESSFUL PARENTING

Few things change our lives more than embarking on the journey of parenthood. As you and your spouse gaze down at that miraculous, tiny little bundle in your arms, you're filled with awe and wonder. When you hear that first newborn cry, you think it must be the sweetest sound you've ever heard.

But as the weeks and months pass, the not-so-glamorous part of childrearing sets in. If you're a parent, you know what I'm talking about. Constant feedings. Endless diaper changes. Sleepless nights. Life as you and your spouse knew it is completely changed.

I remember when my wife and I brought our daughter Karissa home from the hospital. A friend advised, "The best way in the world to ruin your life is going without any sleep. Here's what you do. Put the baby on one end of the house. Then, you sleep at the other end of the house and close as many doors between you and that baby as you can!"

Of course, we didn't follow his advice, but babies do change our lives in a big way. They are a miraculous gift from God, and we have a responsibility to teach them to love, serve, and honor the Lord.

In our culture, children are sometimes seen as more of a curse than a blessing. But biblically, that view is wrong. The Bible says that children are the heritage of the Lord: "Lo, children are an heritage of the LORD: and the fruit of the womb is his reward" (Psalm 127:3). In fact, God promises that it is a happy man who has children: "As arrows are in the hand of a mighty man; so are children of the youth. Happy is the man that hath his quiver full of them: they shall not be ashamed, but they shall speak with the enemies in the gate" (Psalm 127:4–5).

Knowing that children are a gracious and precious gift from God, why do so many Christian parents struggle with raising them?

Well, for starters, parenting is hard work. In fact, the entrance of a new baby in the home can be a significant season of pressure. We don't always think about such a happy occasion as being under pressure. But think of it this way: all of a sudden, you have new decisions to make, unfamiliar stresses, and conflicting advice about the dos and don'ts of raising a baby thrown at you from every possible angle.

But the opportunities and blessings of parenting far outweigh any potential dangers. Armed with advice from God's Word, you can approach parenting biblically from the moment you learn you're expecting.

Before You Start Your Family

Satan likes to take good things, like family and children, and use them as stumbling blocks in our lives. He understands the devastating effect strong Christian families have on one of his biggest missions—to destroy the home. Unfortunately, Christian homes are falling rapidly to his advances.

But that doesn't mean we should throw our hands up in despair and think, "What's the use? I don't have control over how my children turn out anyway." On the contrary, it should encourage us to become more vigilant in our parenting journey.

Back to our earlier question: why do so many Christian parents struggle to raise their children? One of the first reasons is simply that many parents decide to start a family for selfish reasons. Parenting should be a wonderful adventure, but wanting a baby merely for selfish motives places pressure that should never have been there on both parent and child.

Of course, if you are already a parent, you can rest confidently in the truth that God gave you that child. No child is an accident. The Bible is clear on this—God forms a child in the womb with a purpose for that child's life. Consider what God told the prophet Jeremiah: "Before I formed thee in the belly I knew thee; and before thou camest forth out of the womb I sanctified thee, and I ordained thee a prophet unto the nations" (Jeremiah 1:5). Having children from the wrong motives doesn't change the sacredness or purpose of that child's life. It just adds pressure to you and your child and makes an already-challenging endeavor even more difficult.

Of course, as a parent, if you look back and only now recognize unhealthy motives, it's not too late to ask the Lord to help you shift your motives. Whether you already have children or are considering starting your family, search your heart for any of these motives:

First, a wrong reason to have a child is **comparison.** Some couples feel that everyone around them has children, so they should too. Watching parents with their children often creates a natural and understandable desire for a child, but it shouldn't be the only reason we choose to have one. God does not give us children simply so we can be like everyone else. Children are more valuable than to use to keep up with someone else.

Another wrong reason to have a child is only **for the love they can give.** A young married man once told me that he and his wife wanted a child to experience the kind of love that only children can give. There's nothing intrinsically wrong with wanting that innocent, selfless love from a child. In fact, I think that love is something God gave a child. But that love should be an added blessing, not a motive. In fact, our heart as parents should be to *give* love to our children.

Too much emphasis on the love children can give us potentially sets us up for disappointment. What if your child struggles with special needs that keep him from being able to express his love? What if one day your children stop giving you that love when they reach adulthood? What if they rebel and reject you? I hope your children will never do that, but if they do, you will need a stronger foundation in your parent-child relationship than simply wanting to receive their love. Parenting should be the selfless giving of love, not a selfish grab for love.

A third wrong reason to have a child is **to impress others.** That is an unfair burden to place on a child.

Have you ever known a family that pushes their children to extreme excellence—perhaps in music, arts, or sports...or all three—and then shows them off almost like they'd show off a pet? There is nothing wrong with wanting our children to be accomplished and pushing them to grow. But our motive behind that push is important.

Others take pride in how obedient and well behaved their children are. Let me tell you a secret: nobody's children are perfect, and we aren't to place that pressure on our own kids. Biblically, we are to train our children, discipline them, and establish rules in their life. But our motive behind everything that we do as we raise our children is love for them and love for the Saviour. Try this quick test: when you discipline your children, do you do it because you're embarrassed by their behavior, or because you're trying to develop their hearts for God? Your answer reveals a lot about your motive for parenting.

Parents often miss the big picture of parenting when they believe that the pinnacle of successful child rearing is getting their children to obey them. The highest priority we have is teaching our children to obey God, not us. If our children have the right attitude toward the Lord, everything else will take care of itself.

Everything must go back to your heart. If you feel like you have to prove that you and your spouse are perfect parents by how your child behaves or how much he can do, those unrealistic expectations can create bitterness and resentment in your child's heart. Perfection is an impossible standard for any child to live up to.

Fourth, a wrong reason to have a child is **to fill a void in your life.** Jesus Christ is the only person who will satisfy your emptiness. No matter what circumstance you walk through, you are complete in Him (Colossians 2:10).

Throughout the Bible and history, some of the greatest Christians in the world either never married or did marry but never had children.

Children are wonderful, and they often do fill a place in our lives that nothing else can. But you cannot find your worth in having children. God created us with a void in our hearts that nothing but Jesus can fill.

If you are asking the Lord for a child, look at your motives. Does some of your thinking need to be adjusted? Or, if you already have children, have some of those philosophies tainted your view? Ask God to help you shift your thinking to see children through His eyes—created image bearers of God with a special purpose on their lives. And ask Him to help you love and direct your children as He would.

Parenting's Pitfalls

When the angel came to Samson's parents to tell them they were going to have a son, they did not say, "That's great! We're going to have a baby." The first thing they wanted to know was, "How do we rear him?" (Judges 13:10–12).

That is a fantastic question for every parent to ask. From the moment you discover you are expecting a little one, you should begin studying what God's Word says is required of you as a parent. Once again, if you already have children, it's not too late to start studying out what God's Word says about parenting.

Well-meaning parents can develop wrong priorities for their family. Children are precious, and rearing them properly requires an enormous investment of time and energy. But some parents place their children too high on the scale of priorities in their life.

If you find yourself making statements like any of the following, check yourself. You might have the wrong priorities in your life about raising children:

"I am going to spend every moment possible with this child." If you have children, they should be a major priority in your life. Some parents, however, take that to an extreme. They'll say something such as, "I don't take my family to the midweek service anymore. That's our family time." Don't get me wrong—I think family time is important. But the most important thing you can do is teach your children to love God. Part of teaching them love for God is modeling it in our actions. When you think about it, it's difficult to tell them to love God first when you put everything else ahead of Him—including time together as a family. Children will see your real priorities based on your actions, not your words, and make value judgments accordingly. As disciples of Christ, God—not our children—simply must come first in our lives.

"I am going to build my life around this child." God's design is that one day your children will leave your home and pursue the plans He has for them. But if you build your entire life around your children, you'll face a huge letdown when they are gone. A good, godly parent can have other interests. In fact, you should have some. Serve at your church in ministries that you can do with your children and in ministries you can do without them. When our girls were very small, I began preparing my heart for the day that they would leave. I didn't want that day to come—I loved having my children at home. Yet I didn't want to have the mentality of, "Oh, my kids will *always* be around."

"I am never going to let this child out of my sight." One of our most important jobs as parents is to guard our children from the world. But it is physically impossible to guard your children twenty-four hours a day, seven days a week. I have known people who never invited others to their house and never got involved in the ministries of the church so that they could be with their children. That kind of focus will eventually harm your children. Encourage your kids to jump into ministries in the church, form relationships with others in the church (children and adults), and learn to love and serve those around them.

"I am going to shield my child from anything negative." Many parents adopt this mentality in opposition to the idea that parents should expose their children to wrong ideas so they learn how to handle them. Part of this is true. We do have a responsibility to shield our children from these influences. Monitor what television shows your children watch. Know who their friends are. That's part of your responsibility.

But don't go to the opposite extreme. I remember a man who was once a powerful teacher. But now he doesn't believe anyone should teach children except their parents. He doesn't believe in Sunday school or even church. Instead, he promotes *home church*—having "church" with his family at home. That is not shielding your children; that is isolating them. We are not to be *of* the world, but we do have to be *in* it.

To me, my dad's ministry was a great example of proper balance in my childhood. He took over the Detroit City Rescue Mission when I was in first grade. For the next decade, my dad ran that rescue mission. Sometimes, I would get on a bus and ride from my house in the northwest section of Detroit to downtown and walk to the rescue mission. We had camps in the summer, and kids from the inner city and I would hang around those guys who were at the mission in the program. I learned so many things from that experience, and God used it to equip me for ministry. He also used that experience to protect me from sin.

For example, I've yet to taste a drop of an alcoholic beverage. I certainly have regrets from the past, and I struggle with temptation like any Christian. I praise God, however, that drunkenness is not one of them. In a controlled environment, I saw that what the devil delivered was not what he promised.

When I think of ministries that show children the effects of sin, I think of the bus route or a similar ministry. Many needy children whose families have been pillaged by addictions and sin ride church buses. Having a chance to see that up close while at the same time serving these families will show your children that the biggest need of the lost world is Jesus Christ and His deliverance.

Some parents are so committed to shielding their child from anything negative that they will not allow them to fully surrender to God's will. Years ago, a sweet young lady from a family in our church excitedly told her parents, "Mom and Dad, in Christian school chapel today I surrendered my life to God, and I think God wants me to be a missionary!" If your child surrenders to God like this girl did, praise the Lord for that decision! Their plans may change, but never discourage them from obeying God. Unfortunately, this girl's parents told her they weren't going to let her travel to some dangerous place where they couldn't protect her. They didn't want her exposed to danger. Because of her parent's pressure, she decided not to go. Eventually, she married a man of whom her parents approved but who didn't have a strong testimony of commitment to Christ. After they had been married just a few months and were expecting a baby, he walked out on her, leaving her to raise their child on her own.

Your children are not yours to keep. They are not just for you to shelter from everything you think is bad. They are for you to rear to serve God.

The best way to protect your children is give them to the Lord and let Him decide where they are to go. This runs contrary to our natural impulse as parents, but your children are better off in the most dangerous jungle in the will of God than they are in the safest American city outside the will of God. It's not your job to put them in the safest environment you can imagine; it's your job to point them to the will of God.

"If I teach my children to obey, that is enough." Your children need more than rules; they need a relationship with you. Beyond just training them to do right, you need to express your love and affirmation in their lives. Your children need to know that you love them through your words and actions. They in turn will respond with love to your correction.

What if I went next door and corrected my neighbors' children? They (not to mention the parents) would be furious because I had no relationship or right to correct them. Discipline without a loving relationship is often ineffective and sometimes even harmful. But a loving relationship combined with consistent, biblical discipline is a recipe for successful childrearing.

There are common pitfalls parents and potential parents may experience, and we have to be on guard. But let's get more specific. How do we raise our children? What is the true reason God gives us children?

Passing It on to the Next Generation

Most parents desire to see their children succeed as adults. And most Christian parents want their children to have a heart to serve God. What some fail to recognize, however, is that these objectives require work.

May I be blunt? Parents everywhere (even Christians) are rearing a generation of pampered, protected, coddled, self-centered brats who think the world revolves around them. They refuse to correct their child when their child is young, assuming he'll still turn out well. But when that child becomes a sullen, rebellious adult or teenager, parents wonder what happened.

Worldly methods of parenting will never produce good results. Many people like the end product of godly parenting, but they shy away when they realize how much effort it requires.

We can see in Psalm 127 that children are a heritage, but think about what that means.

In 1897, my great-great-grandfather gave my great-grandfather an Elgin pocket watch. It is gold-filled and came with a twenty-year guarantee. The inscription says,

"February 18, 1897, given to Albert Boch by his parents." When I wear a suit with a vest, I often wear that watch. Before my grandmother died, she gave my mother the watch, and my mother gave it to me. Although the watch is over a century old, I want to pass it down to my first grandson.

Like that watch, children are not just for you; they are for you to pass on to the next generation. Think about it. If you have a daughter, you may be rearing your future son-in-law's wife. If you have a son, you may be rearing your future daughter-in-law's husband. If you have children, you could be rearing your grandchildren's parents. Raising your children is not for you and your needs and desires. It is about preparing the next generation.

If a heritage is something given to a person to continue to pass on from generation to generation, it's not something for which we can take credit. This is key to grasp for successful parenting—your children are not for you to keep. They are for you to rear to give back to God and equip for His service. In Psalm 127:4, we see that children are described as arrows. This is an incredible word picture.

In Bible times, an arrow extended the ability of a soldier far beyond his reach. Most weapons, such as swords, are limited in their impact on the enemy to the length of the arm of the soldier. But arrows greatly increased the ability of a soldier to strike. Likewise, your children extend your life and ministry far beyond what you will be able to do in your own lifetime.

I recently read about the violin that Joshua Bell, one of the world's top violinists, plays. Made by the master violin-maker, Stradivarius, in 1713, the violin cost Joshua Bell millions of dollars because of the incredible sound it produces. That's amazing—nearly three hundred years of use has not diminished the value of the violin—in fact, it has increased it.

This is true of parenting as well. You can train your children to be used by God even more than you are. Your children will then train your grandchildren, and your grandchildren will train your great-grandchildren to still walk in His paths. What a weighty, awesome responsibility!

Children are given to us as a temporary trust—not ours to keep, but ours to raise for just a little while until they reach adulthood.

Just as we might entrust the care of our children to someone else if something were to happen to us, that is what God has asked us to do. He has given us children to train for Him. They never have and never will belong to us—they belong to God.

Picture the arrow illustration in your mind again. From the experience I've had with archery, I can tell you that the arrow does not always go where I want it to go. It goes where I aim it. While I've missed the target a few times, the fault is never in the arrow. It is the fault of the archer in how he aimed the arrow. Likewise, our children will go in the direction we aim them as parents. Of course, unlike arrows, God has given every human a free will, and sometimes, our children will choose to go another direction. But our role in pointing them toward God—especially when they are young—is crucial.

The Priority of Biblical Parenting

We know it should be a priority in our lives to raise our children for the Lord. But how do we do that? What plan does God lay out in Scripture?

First, God requires that we train our child. Proverbs 22:6 says, "Train up a child in the way he should go: and when he is old, he will not depart from it." The Hebrew word translated *train* is the word for sharpening something like an axe or a sword. It implies a careful and repeated process of honing to reach the desired result. Biblical child training is not a casual or occasional process. It requires repetition, consistency, and love.

This takes diligence. There will be times when the last thing that you want to do is train your child. But God blesses parents who are consistent. As you ask the Lord for help, and, as you spend time in His Word daily, He will give you discernment and wisdom in rearing the children He has given to you.

Not only does God call us to train our children, but He instructs us to raise them in the nurture and admonition of the Lord. Ephesians 6:4 says, "And, ye fathers, provoke not your children to wrath: but bring them up in the nurture and admonition of the Lord."

Having a child enter your life is one of the most dramatic transitions you will face. When you're walking through that transition, make sure you remain faithful to the Lord. If you were reading the Bible every day before, make sure you read the Bible every day now. If you were faithful to church, keep going now. If you were involved in a ministry, continue serving. It's key that instead of allowing children to dominate our life, we *add* them to our life.

By continuing to faithfully serve the Lord after we have children, we set a godly example for them. When Karissa was young, I asked advice from a man who'd done a good job rearing his children. I was surprised to hear him tell me that he was scared all the time. By this, he meant that he was afraid that he would do something that would lead his children away from God. We want our children to know that we live what we teach.

The pattern in the Bible is to teach your children throughout the day "…when thou sittest in thine house, and when thou walkest by the way, and when thou liest down, and when thou risest up" (Deuteronomy 6:7). Constantly be in a teaching mode. Show your children the truths of the Word of God. Take advantage of things that happen to show them from the Bible what God says about what they have seen and heard.

As you train your children, keep in mind that they should be secondary to your relationship with your spouse and the Lord. Precious as they are, children can be an incredible distraction! Maintaining a good relationship with God and your spouse requires purpose. On a practical level, that might mean getting a baby sitter and going out to eat as a couple. That relationship with your spouse will last beyond the time when your children leave home, and you need to be investing in your marriage on a daily basis.

One of the best ways to grow together as a family is serving God together. Yet too often, I find that people feel as if they need to choose between God and their family. While I think you should have fun and relaxing times as a family, it is vital that your children be involved in the work of God with you.

I'm thankful I grew up in the work of God. As I mentioned, my dad ran the Detroit Rescue Mission, and every Sunday afternoon we would have lunch there, eating the same food the men at the mission ate. After lunch, we'd hold a service, and I'd always be involved. Sometimes, I'd lead the singing. Other times I'd play my trumpet. Growing up in that background, it never seemed to me to be a strange thing to serve God. Years later, I never wanted my daughters to think it was a strange thing to serve the Lord.

They've never had to ask if we're going to church, even on vacation. We were always faithful to the Lord's house.

Ever since our daughters were babies, Krisy and I took them with us out soulwinning. We wanted them to learn that witnessing and serving God are a privilege we have as His children.

It doesn't take much time in the world to realize that we live in an extremely selfish society. Children must learn that not everything in life is about them. Instead, they need to give of themselves. They must serve others.

Years ago, I was preparing to preach at a church when I met a little boy, about nine or ten years old, whose job was to put the water on the pulpit for the speaker. He said, "Brother Ouellette, how do you like your water? Do you like it with ice or without ice?" Someone had taught the boy that it is a big deal to do something for God and for the servants of God. What an incredible lesson to teach your children! The ultimate goal of parenting is preparing your children to make godly, wise choices when they become adults.

The Privilege of Parenting

Having children is a privilege. There are many people who would love to have children, but have been unable to. I understand that pain. I remember begging God for years for a child. Finally, after ten years of marriage, we adopted a daughter. Five years later, our second daughter was born. I personally understand what it is like to desperately want a child, and it grieves me when I hear people say things such as, "Oh, these children! I don't know what I'm going to do with them. I can't wait for school to start."

Our attitude should never be to get rid of our children or get by with the least amount of parenting we can. They are a precious gift.

Parenting is the adventure of a lifetime. It reveals much about who we are, our heart motives, and just how much we still have to learn. Whether you're just now embarking on the journey of parenthood or you've been on it for several years, there are always areas to grow in. Ask God for wisdom. Seek out wise counsel. Make adjustments as you grow in your walk with God, understanding of His Word, and wisdom as a parent. Above all, pray for your children—that they would know God, love God, and fulfil His plan for their lives.

Parenting the children God has entrusted to your care may be demanding—even stressful at times—but it is an incredible privilege.

FIVE

NAVIGATING THE TEEN YEARS

I heard the story of a teenager who came home with a completely different hairstyle. The sides of her head were shaved, the rest of her hair was died burgundy, and the top was spiked. The girl's mother, trying to mask her shock, said, "That's a bit different, isn't it?"

Later, a friend saw the haircut and asked, "What does your mom think of it?"

"Oh, my mom's pretty cool," the girl answered. "She doesn't mind at all."

"Then why did you even do it?" her bewildered friend asked.

Teenagers can be challenging to understand. If you're the parent of young children, you've probably heard the groans and seen the eye rolls from friends who are parents of teens as they tell you, "You have it so easy. Just wait until they become teenagers."

But while raising teenagers is a pressure point of life, it doesn't automatically equal six years of misery. It doesn't mean you throw up your hands in despair, cross your fingers, and just hope your teenage kids will turn out right.

On the contrary, when we couple biblical truth with a practical understanding of the teen years, raising teenagers can be a sweet time of fellowship with our children as they approach adulthood. In this chapter, we'll look at actions we can take to help our children navigate the problems and issues of the teen years and how we can help guide them into becoming responsible adults that love the Lord.

Child or Adult?

There are only two categories of people mentioned in the Bible—children and adults. There are no references in God's Word to tweenagers or teenagers. Instead, those are terms society uses to identify and categorize people by their age. While it's not wrong to call someone a teenager, much of what we normally associate with the word isn't a biblical concept. We need to be on guard against adopting society's wrong philosophies and approaches toward being a teenager. Doing something just because society says to do it isn't right.

In fact, the word *teenager* wasn't even a societal concept until relatively recently. Author and researcher Robert Epstein, who wrote the book *The Case Against Adolescence: Rediscovering the Adult in Every Teen*, said this:

> Unfortunately, the dramatic changes set in motion by the turmoil of America's industrial revolution also obliterated from modern consciousness the true abilities of young people, leaving adults with the faulty belief that teenagers were inherently irresponsible and incompetent. What's more, the rate at which restrictions were placed on young people began to accelerate after the 1930s and increased dramatically after the social turmoil of the 1960s. Surveys I've conducted suggest that teenagers today are subject to ten times as many restrictions as are mainstream adults, to twice as many restrictions as are active-duty U.S. Marines, and even to twice as many restrictions as are incarcerated felons."[1]

Today, many seem to excuse, accept, and even encourage irresponsibility and immaturity in young people. Teenagers are not children anymore and

---

[1] Robert Epstein, "Let's Abolish High School." *Edweek.org*, April 3. 2007, https://www.edweek.org/ew/articles/2007/04/04/31epstein.h26.html (accessed June 21, 2018).

should not be treated as if they are incapable of making responsible decisions. On the other hand, neither should we go to the other extreme and give teenagers complete independence. I've heard people say things such as, "Well, I just think that when they become teenagers, they should make their own decisions," or, "Well, you know that once they're teenagers, you just can't tell them what to do all the time," or, "We don't want to restrict them too much, because if we did they'd probably just get mad and run away."

Both extremes—too much independence or too little independence—are harmful. The key to successfully parenting teens is using a balanced approach from Scripture.

What Happened? And Who Is This Person Living in My House?

Our children go through stages of growing up. First, our child is a tiny baby we bring home from the hospital. Then, our child grows into a cute elementary school kid that we hug and kiss goodnight. But one morning, we wake up to discover that some alien from outer space has inhabited our child's body. He doesn't want to kiss or hug us anymore. He doesn't want to tell us about his day. He doesn't like wrestling on the floor anymore. The reason? He's entered the teen years.

You ask, "What happened? Did I do something wrong? How should I respond?" Short answer, you didn't do anything. For the next several years, your child will begin going through a period of dramatic change. The transition into adulthood can affect your child's behaviors.

Teenagers are gradually becoming more independent. They like to do things on their own without parental help. When I was thirteen, I remember my dad asking me, "Son, you're growing up, and you're getting some whiskers. Would you like me to show you how to shave?"

I responded, "No. I already know how." Because I had watched a Gillette commercial on television, I figured that I wouldn't need any help shaving. And you know, 732 Band-Aids later, I did finally figure it out.

Slowly, teenagers are becoming less dependent on the help and opinions of their parents. If you tell your seven- or eight-year-old, "I don't think that sweater looks good with those pants," he will likely go get another one. But try telling that to your seventeen-year-old. Most likely, your teen will look at you like you're an idiot. Slowly, teenagers develop their own style and preferences.

I remember one time my mother gave our daughter Karissa an expensive watch. For some reason, Karissa put it on her right hand. My mother replied, "No, sweetie, that goes on your left hand." Karissa said, "I want to wear it on my right hand." They went back and forth for quite a while simply because Karissa wanted to wear the watch her own way.

Teenagers are determined to become their own individuals. As a result, it may be more difficult for them to accept your counsel and advice.

Teenagers are starting to communicate less. Younger children may want to tell you *everything* that happened during the day while they were at school—from the moment they got on the bus to lunchtime to the ride home. But sometimes, it can seem impossible to get teenagers to say or do anything beyond greet you. They don't want to tell you about school, friends, projects—you fill in the blank. Slowly, they are drawing more into themselves and their age group.

If your teenagers begin to act differently, it's often because they're going through a period of insecurity as they try to figure out how adults relate with one another. As a result, they may struggle with affection and expressing their thoughts. I have been a pastor for years, and I've noticed how eager little children are to run up and give me a hug. But as far as teenagers go—well, let's just say that it's been a long time since a big, strapping, teenage boy ran up to me in the hall and gave me a hug. They still love our church, but their responses and the way they express themselves have changed.

I've heard people say, "Young people are living in the best time of their life. Those were the golden years. What have they got to worry about?"

I couldn't disagree more. Remember when you were a teenager? You would reach for a glass of milk, but your arm had grown two inches since the last time you picked up a glass. In fact, you ended up spilling the whole thing. You felt like your face was one large zit, and your parents should have bought stock in Clearasil. Personally, I wouldn't want to be a teenager again for anything. No wonder teenagers are so worried about fitting in—everything in their life is changing.

When your children are little, you are their whole world. Almost all that a baby knows is his mom and dad. Parents are the ones who feed him, hug him, burp him, and change him. While he's aware that there are other people in the world, he is absolutely dependent on his parents. In fact, he couldn't make it without them. But by the time that child becomes a teenager the parent is only part of his world (and sometimes, not even the most important part). Suddenly, outside opinions matter greatly.

When Karissa was in the first grade, I remember her returning home from school with a question. I answered, but she replied, "No, Dad, that's not the answer. That's not what my teacher said."

I gently told her that the teacher might be mistaken.

Karissa looked shocked. "No, Dad! Miss Hintz said that wasn't the answer!"

That day it dawned on me. Our first daughter was in first grade. She was not going to believe everything I said all the time anymore. I was no longer the only source of knowledge in her life.

Teens are more concerned about their peers' opinions than those of their parents. Because of that, they're motivated to sometimes do strange things. They want to follow the latest fashion trend, even if you think it completely clashes. If that's what everyone else is doing, they want to be part of it.

Teenagers experience a complicated time in their life. They're figuring out who they are and what they want to do with their life. This can potentially be an awkward transition phase—certainly for the teenager, but also for the parent.

One difference between you and your teenager, however, is that you do not have to feed off of their insecurity. Do your best to understand them and love them, but don't take their confusion and frustrations personally.

Avoiding the Control Trap

As a parent, you want your child to turn out right. You passionately love your child, and you want to be part of his life. Those are both noble and biblical goals. In Scripture, we see a serious responsibility to guide our children to love and serve God.

Don't fall into the trap, however, of exercising excessive and unnecessary control. In your desire for your child to turn out right, you should do your best not to micromanage your child's life. One of the crucial areas in which your teenager needs to mature is in the ability to make right choices independently of you. Part of that is turning them loose to make decisions on their own.

Giving them independence does not mean allowing our children the freedom to sin. Nor does it mean letting them to do things we believe may physically harm them. It means that we permit our children to choose between what is good and acceptable. Teach your children that there are consequences when they make a wrong choice—then allow them to suffer those consequences. If we protect our children every time from things that aren't the best choice, they'll have trouble discerning what wise choices are.

The best way to find balance is asking the Lord for discernment between what is preference and what is sin.

When you disagree with your teenager, ask yourself why you disagree. If it's a biblical reason, you should tell your child "no" as their God-given authority and even explain the Scriptural truth on which you are basing your decision. Occasionally, there may be times when you can't point to a specific principle, but have an unsettledness in your spirit over allowing them to participate in an activity or an event or perhaps even to develop close relationships with certain people. It's okay to tell your son or daughter that is why you are saying "no" and to ask them to trust you with it. Generally speaking, however, it's best if you can give them biblical principles upon which they can make future decisions.

If, however, you disagree with them because of a difference in preferences, consider allowing them room to express their individual taste and style. For example, if one of my daughters wanted to wear a shirt that just wasn't my personal taste, I would let them wear the shirt. But if one of my daughters wanted to wear a shirt that I felt was immodest, I would not allow them to do so. Your children don't have to adopt your exact preferences in order to be good and godly children.

Some parents, however, go to the opposite extreme and don't express appropriate control. Because they're weary of constantly battling their child, they give up and allow him to do whatever he wants. In reality, parents that do so are taking the easy way out by letting their child make wrong, sinful decisions.

Never allow your children to do things that you know are wrong. Even if everybody at school is doing something unbiblical, refuse to allow your teen to participate. Don't compromise on what is right and wrong. Set and enforce rules for everyone who lives in your house.

As you're enforcing rules, however, the tone and demeanor you adopt will go a long way toward determining how your child responds. I remind the parents in our church, "How I present truth in the pulpit and how I present truth to my children or in the counseling office are entirely different." Don't "preach" at your child.

Some parents seem to think they need to keep on saying something until the child agrees, at least verbally. The problem with that approach is there is an "OFF" switch in the mind of the teenager that is automatically set to trip about thirty seconds into a lecture. It is difficult to reach your child by repeating a lecture over and over again. Instead, make your point briefly and clearly.

Remember how we said teenagers often show little affection? Never let that stop you from showing affection back. If your mailbox responds more to a hug than your teenager does, hug him anyway. You may think that you are simply doing what your teenager wants by not showing affection when, in reality, your lack of outward affection makes your teenager think that he is no longer loved by you.

Mrs. John R. Rice used to say, "Love, unexpressed, dies." This is not to say that you should embarrass your fifteen-year-old son by kissing him in public. But continue to show your love both verbally and physically, even after your children become teenagers. Find ways to let them know that you still care. Remember, teenagers are insecure and need to be reassured that your love is unchanging.

Some parents forget the emotions of the teenage years. When I was in middle school, other students had what they called a "Slam Book." Students would take turns writing down what they thought of others. I remember the day that I read what was written on my page. Some students had made fun of my clothes. My father was running the Detroit City Rescue Mission, and all my clothes came from the mission. We didn't have money for anything else. I hadn't paid a lot of attention to my clothing until then, but at that moment, I would have done anything—good or bad, right or wrong—to be accepted by my peers. I eventually grew out of that insecurity over my clothes, but at the time it was very real.

When your teens struggle with rejection, isolation, or other problems, take their emotions seriously. They are real to them just as they were real to us. Don't let your estimation of the size of their problem influence how you respond.

Nurturing Our Children

When we use the word *nurture*, we generally think it's synonymous with comforting. While that is part of the definition, the root of the word as used in Ephesians 6:4—"bring them up in the nurture and admonition of the Lord"—implies correction and instruction in the truth.

It's our responsibility to ensure our children know what is right. We have a crucial responsibility to nurture our children in the Lord. How do we nurture teens? Here are three ways:

We nurture by teaching our children all the time, wherever we are. Be cautious about thinking that because you put your children in a Christian school, send them on church youth activities, or take them to Sunday school, you've done your job. All those things are wonderful tools to help raise your children, but they do not replace the training you must do. They are supplements, not substitutes. Deuteronomy 6 instructs us to always be teaching our children, no matter where we are or what we are doing: "And these words, which I command thee this day, shall be in thine heart: And thou shalt teach them diligently unto thy children, and shalt talk of them when thou sittest in thine house, and when thou walkest by the way, and when thou liest down, and when thou risest up. And thou shalt bind them for a sign upon thine hand, and they shall be as frontlets between thine eyes. And thou shalt write them upon the posts of thy house, and on thy gates" (Deuteronomy 6:6–9).

We nurture by teaching them truth. It is much easier to teach your children what is right and true than to try to expose everything that is wrong. I have read that the Chinese banking families would let their very young children play with real money. They never showed them counterfeit money. By the time they were old enough to work at the bank, they were so familiar with the real money that they could instantly recognize counterfeit currency.

The best defense against error is not to study every variation of error that is in the world, but to study the truth. If your children know the truth intimately and personally, errors won't hold the same appeal. Remember how Jesus responded to Satan's temptation? He answered every challenge by quoting the Scriptures because He knew the truth. He said in Matthew 4:4, "...*It is written*, Man shall not live by bread alone, but by every word that proceedeth out of the mouth of God."

As parents, we can create a great atmosphere for discussing truth. It could be as simple as an informal conversation over dinner at the table. It can come through family devotion time as you open the Word of God with your family. When your teens come to you for advice, don't just give them an answer, but steer them towards God's Word and the answers found inside.

We nurture by admonishing them. Admonition specifically refers to calling attention to something. When your children fail to use good manners, remind them. If they're disrespectful, correct them. Beyond that, however, teach them right behavior. It's of little use to them if all they know is what is wrong, not what is right.

Admonition outside the context of nurturing is a recipe for resentment and rebellion. Rules without relationship lead to rebellion.

When you correct and admonish your teenagers, don't provoke them to wrath. Ephesians 6:4 commands, "And, ye fathers, provoke not your children to wrath: but bring them up in the nurture and admonition of the Lord." An easy way to provoke your children to wrath is constantly nagging them or arbitrarily asserting your authority. All of God's commands in the Bible are important, but I believe the negative commands (the "thou shalt not" commands) carry greater weight and importance. "Provoke not your children" is a negative command, and it is critical to maintaining a wholesome relationship with them.

Not provoking them to wrath does not mean that they will never be angered over your rules or the boundaries you set for them. But it does mean that you should not be doing it in a manner or attitude that is personal, vindictive, or unreasonable.

As Christians, we are commanded to be kind—even when our children seem to drive us crazy. Always treat your children with respect and kindness, even when you are disciplining them or when they disagree with you. Try to make it your goal that they never walk away feeling like they have been treated disrespectfully. They shouldn't be able to honestly complain about your disposition and demeanor, even if they complain about your decision.

While it is important to treat any child with respect, it is especially true for teenagers. For example, I rarely raise my voice with teenagers. I want to speak to them just as I would speak to an adult. As parents, our job is to protect our children, not hurt them. Don't call them names or belittle them. Don't point out their faults in public. Don't try to embarrass them.

Always remember that teenagers are unsure of themselves. When you speak to them with respect, it makes it easier for them to show you the proper respect in return. They are less likely to immediately shut down your correction because of how you corrected them. In addition, their heart is prepared to listen to what you have to say.

It's easier to provoke our children to wrath if we discipline when we are frustrated with them. During those times, you're more likely to say the wrong thing or to say the right thing in the wrong way. Teenagers will remember your tone and word choices just as much as, if not more than, they remember the actual lesson you're trying to convey. Provoking your children to wrath will breed rebellion in your child's life.

At this point, you may be thinking, *Wait a minute. Shouldn't my children obey me just because I said so?* You're right—children are responsible to obey. But I've found that you'll get a much better response if you're careful about how you express your authority. If you are arbitrarily throwing your weight around, you are likely provoking your children's anger. Your children don't deserve an explanation before they obey, but do try to always have a biblical, thought-out reason for what you do. We taught our daughters, "First you obey; then we explain." As your children grow older, they need you to explain to them the reason behind their rules. In doing so, your children will internalize what you are trying to teach them. Because they have the foundation of "why," it is easier for them to carry those biblical beliefs and precepts with them into adulthood.

Communicating with Teens

Every teen is different, but most go through at least a season of struggling in communication. But there are practical ideas you can follow to help keep the communication lines open.

Put yourself in their shoes. Remember what it felt like when you were a teenager? Put yourself in your teen's position. Emotions are very close to the surface and very real to teens, and you need to try to identify with those emotions as you talk to them.

Ask God to help you understand what teenagers are thinking. Pray for wisdom to discern their real issues. Frequently, they will not tell you the real concern they have at first. That's why it's vital to encourage them to keep talking until you uncover the root issue.

One way to do this is telling them how you felt as a teenager. Many teenagers think they are the only ones who have ever felt the way they do. Simply finding out that someone else has been through similar issues is comforting. In addition, talking through your experiences also helps you to empathize with and remember their struggles and emotions.

Ask your teenager questions that lead to the truth you want them to see. It is important that your teen recognizes you're trying to understand where he is coming from. It may be tough for you to relate. It may feel like you're on completely different wavelengths. But your teen needs to feel like you're trying. When teenagers recognize that you're taking time to "get it," they'll be more prepared mentally to listen to instruction or advice that you have to give.

Keep showing love. Do this appropriately, but faithfully. Teenagers sometimes struggle with expressing love to their parents. As a result, parents stop showing affection because their child has stopped returning it. Then, when the child wants to receive love again, the parent is out of habit. Continue to say, "I love you," even if all you get is a grunt in return.

Things are changing very rapidly for teenagers. They need to know that there is a constant and unchanging love from their parents that they can count on. It may be several years before they acknowledge it, but if you continue to verbalize and show your love, it will greatly help them to stay on the right path.

Don't be a drill sergeant. That does not mean that you do not deal with your teen when he does wrong, but it does mean that you do not make a federal capital case out of a misdemeanor. There are times when your children need to see you grieve, and there may even be times when they need to see you angry, but this should be reserved for truly serious matters.

Many times parents overreact because they are embarrassed by what the child has done instead of responding with appropriate severity to the actual offense. Teenagers are acutely aware of this kind of hypocrisy. It's hard for them to respect a parent who is upset over being embarrassed rather than over what was done wrong.

Set a standard. Set the rules and consequences ahead of time so that the child knows the consequences of the choice. Then, simply enforce the appropriate penalty when the rule is broken. By doing this, you eliminate much of the drama and fighting that often accompanies punishment.

When I did wrong, my father used to sit across from me and ask, "What did you do?"

After I told him, he would say, "And what did we say was going to happen if you did (or didn't do) that?" Again, I would supply my own noose for the hanging. Then, he would simply enforce whatever the punishment was.

Because of the way he handled it, I had nothing to be upset over. While I didn't like the process, I knew it was fair.

Ask God for help. If you are dealing with a difficult teenager, set aside fifteen minutes a day when you do nothing but pray for him. That's much harder than it sounds. Praying specifically for one thing for fifteen minutes requires focus and discipline. Enter into spiritual warfare on behalf of your child.

Pray that God will turn your child's heart toward Him. Ephesians 6:12 says, "For we wrestle not against flesh and blood, but against principalities, against powers, against the rulers of the darkness of this world, against spiritual wickedness in high places." God will do amazing things if you are faithful to pray.

The Terrible Teens?

In your home, the phrase, "the terrible teens" doesn't have to be true. Society has twisted the teenage years into something like a storm to ride out. Does raising teenagers have its challenges? Of course. But so does any other stage of life. I've found that, if you'll incorporate biblical truth in your parenting, your teens can become not just your children, but your friends. The teenage years don't have to be a miserable time for you and your spouse.

When your child turns thirteen, continue seeking God's face for wisdom. Be prepared to give lots of unconditional love. Recognize that your child is gradually growing into an adult. With the Lord's help, it is possible to successfully navigate the teen years.

SIX

HELPING YOUR CHILD THROUGH STRUGGLES

Have you ever met a self-appointed parenting expert? The expert feels that it's his duty to tell you *exactly* what you're doing wrong in your parenting and how you could do better. I've noticed a common trait among these experts: they either don't have children or their children are very young. As they're giving advice, they don't stop to consider that their perfect four-year-old might one day turn into a rebellious teen.

While we probably don't take the words of the self-appointed parenting expert very seriously, haven't all of us had a moment or two where we wondered if we were doing this whole parenting thing right? Have you ever asked yourself, "How do I make sure my children turn out right?"

All Christian parents should desire for their children to become godly, Christ-focused adults, living out God's purposes for their lives. We want our children to become adults who love and serve the Lord. But the reality is that every child will have times of struggle along the way—just as we adults have times of struggle.

My wife and I didn't have children right away. In fact, we were married for ten years before we adopted a baby girl. During the time we didn't have children, I watched what parents around me did. I saw many things I wanted to copy, but I also saw many things I wanted to avoid.

Looking back, I see that delay as a blessing from the Lord. Yes, it was difficult at times watching other parents with children when my wife and I wanted a child so badly. Yet God knew that I would be a better father later in my life than I would have been earlier.

All of us know we could grow in our parenting. But there are seasons when we feel our inadequacy more acutely. In fact, you may be reading this chapter as your child is even now going through a season of struggle. You may be wondering if you're failing as a parent or if this is normal or if there is something you can change or if there is any hope at all.

The Bible tells us in Proverbs 22:6, "Train up a child in the way he should go: and when he is old, he will not depart from it." Over the next few pages, we're going to look closer at this word *train*. While I don't pretend to have all the answers, I want to share with you biblical principles I've learned through studying God's Word and raising my children. It's my prayer that, by the end of this chapter, you'll be armed with practical, biblical ideas to help your struggling child.

A God-Given Responsibility

Every profession has responsibilities. Doctors have the responsibility to care for their patients. Lawyers have the responsibility to prepare for cases. Store-owners have the responsibility to keep their inventory stocked. Think with me of parenting as a profession. We have a responsibility to teach our children to do right.

Training our children is a phrase we frequently use. But what does it mean? What are the responsibilities that come with training our children?

Parents have a responsibility to protect their children. I have heard parents say, "Well, I want my child to know what the world is really like. If you keep them sheltered, they won't know what to do when they go out on their own. You're raising greenhouse Christians."

At first, that philosophy sounds reasonable. But it actually contradicts the Bible. A verse that is instructive here is Romans 16:19: "For your obedience is come abroad unto all men. I am glad therefore on your behalf: but yet I would have you wise unto that which is good, and simple concerning evil."

The word *simple* in this verse means to be unaware. This does not mean that we should raise naïve children, but rather children who have a strong grasp on what is holy, true, and right. God does not want your children (or you for that matter) to be exposed to evil in order to learn how to handle it. We are to be separated from the world (James 1:27), not trying to see how involved with it we can be without actually sinning.

When I was a boy, we lived on Main Street in Perry, Michigan. What would happen if, as a little boy, I took my toy car outside to play and decided that the paved road was better than the grass because the car would go further? One thing I can tell you for a fact is that my mother would not begin calmly lecturing me on the Department of Transportation. She wouldn't carefully explain the laws of physics to describe what would happen if a car hit me. Instead, she would yell, "Stop! Get out! It's not safe for you to be there!" She would be a poor mother if she allowed me to learn the dangers of the road through experience.

It takes discipline to protect our children, especially as they grow older. Just because you have teenagers doesn't mean you practice a hands-off mentality. I know parents of teenagers who never ask who else is going to be at the house where their children are going or if they're going to go anywhere else while they're out. The responsibility for protection does not end on the thirteenth birthday.

Parents have a responsibility to correct their children. Many of us could tell stories of children turning their back on the Lord. When that happens, it's easy to shift blame to a church, a school, a teacher, or a leader such as a pastor or youth pastor. But Proverbs 22:15 says, "Foolishness is bound in the heart of a child; but the rod of correction shall drive it far from him." Do you catch what this verse is saying? It's not school that corrupts children. It's not the neighbor's kid who teaches them how to lie. It's not failure on the part of the Sunday school teacher. It is the child's heart that is already corrupt.

How, then, do we help a wayward child? Fundamentally, we must recognize that a child will not grow better on his own. In fact, Proverbs 29:15 says, "The rod and reproof give wisdom: but a child left to himself bringeth his mother to shame." Based on this verse, you must take steps to point out, give correction, and stop the bad behavior of your children. If you do not correct them, you are heading for trouble.

When parenting gets tough, we have to recognize that it is part of our child's fleshly nature to resist correction. Keep doing it—they need you to correct them. Sometimes, when I speak in Christian school chapels, I talk to students about the responsibility of their parents to correct them. To illustrate, I sometimes ask them how many still suck their thumbs. Nobody has ever yet admitted to that. Then, I point out that it was likely their parents who taught them to not suck their thumbs. They needed correction then, and they still need it as teens. We need to correct our children and drive out the folly bound in their hearts.

Parents have a responsibility to perfect their children. Correcting our children is a start, but we also need to perfect them. Ephesians 6:4 says, "And, ye fathers, provoke not your children to wrath: but bring them up in the nurture and admonition of the Lord."

In this verse, the word *nurture* means "tutoring," and the word *admonition* means "to call attention to." The word refers to a mild rebuke or warning. Both nurturing and admonishing are essential. You must not only warn your children when they do wrong, you must build them up so that they will do right. This is a vital part of the training process.

My friend Dr. Curtis Hutson told about a time when his son didn't clean up his room. His wife said, "I trained him better than that."

Dr. Hutson gently replied, "No, you *told* him. If you had trained him, he would have cleaned his room."

There's a crucial difference between telling and training. Many parents have told their children to do right, but they do not insist on proper performance. Ultimately, it becomes a contest of wills. As the process drags on, many parents give up, and the results are disastrous.

We need to perfect our children. This doesn't mean we need perfect children; it means we need to help them get to the place where they are doing the things we have been teaching them. The biblical use of the word *perfect* carries the sense of completion—having everything that is needed.

One of the most important jobs we have is training and rearing our children to glorify God. That's a grave responsibility and an awesome privilege. If we nurture and admonish our children, while our children may have seasons of struggle, we can look forward to them following the Lord as they grow older.

A Bible Principle

At the beginning of the chapter, we looked at Proverbs 22:6, "Train up a child in the way he should go: and when he is old, he will not depart from it."

Maybe that verse struck you as uncomfortable. To the best of your knowledge, you are training your child to follow God. But it doesn't seem like it's working. Your child is willfully rebelling against you, and you don't know what to change. I get that. Frankly, Christians debate the meaning of this verse. Is it a promise, or is it a principle? (Sometimes, it seems like a parent's view of this verse is determined by how well his children turn out.)

From a contextual standpoint, I believe that the book of Proverbs in Scripture is primarily presented as principles. These are observations of what is generally true, not promises of what God will do. Of course, as the very Word of God, every verse in Proverbs is true. But it should not be used outside of the context in which it is given to us.

One of the ways we can discern if we are accurately interpreting Scripture is to compare it with other passages. For instance, Romans 14:12 says, "So then every one of us shall give account of himself to God." Every person has to take personal responsibility for his actions. You can't blame a child's failure entirely on the parents.

Some people grow up in a good home, have good training, and still willfully and deliberately choose to do wrong and go away from God. I have a friend who went to a Christian school with two boys from the same family. Today, one of them is a Christian school principal; the other is serving a life sentence for murder.

As a general rule, however, if a child is trained to do right, he will continue to do right once he reaches adulthood. If that principle were not generally true, God would not have placed it in the Bible.

How we rear our children does make a difference. Even if it seems like your children don't understand or disagree with everything you say, don't grow discouraged and stop trying. When I attended Bible college, there were things the administration did that I disagreed with. But over time, I came to agree with many of their positions, especially when I entered the ministry myself and had a better perspective of where they were coming from.

Since the Fall, all of us are born sinners. That means that even if we properly train our children, they may still do wrong. And as humans, just like us, they *will* have seasons of struggle. What do we do during those times?

Harmful Responses

How we respond when our children struggle can make a challenging situation better or worse. Furthermore, a wise response isn't necessarily intuitive as we might think it would be. In fact, Scripture records two fathers who were God-fearing men but didn't respond well when their children got into trouble.

Eli and His Sons—As the high priest, Eli was the top leader in the nation of Israel. He was the one to whom the people looked for both spiritual and secular guidance. He was the mouthpiece of God. He offered the sacrifices that were a type of the Lamb of God who would come to pay for the sins of the world. This was a man who was widely respected and who loved the Lord. Unfortunately, his sons did not follow the God of their father. As we look at 1 Samuel 2, we see that God brought two charges against Eli's sons.

First, Eli's sons desecrated the sacrifice. First Samuel 2:17 says, "Wherefore the sin of the young men was very great before the LORD: for men abhorred the offering of the LORD."

God's plan of provision for the priests was that they would receive part of the sacrifices for their own food. But rather than be content with their allotted portion, Hophni and Phinehas took the best cuts of meat for themselves. They took something that was supposed to be a joyous time as the people of God brought their offerings and turned it into an occasion to satisfy their appetites.

Things grew so bad that people hated going to the tabernacle and giving their sacrifices. What an incredible defilement against the testimony of God! Many of us could attest to our own experience with men like Eli's sons. We've seen spiritual leaders leave the ministry in disgrace because of moral or financial sins.

But stealing sacrifices was just the beginning of Eli's sons' wickedness. The second charge against Eli's sons was that they defiled the tabernacle. First Samuel 2:22 says, "Now Eli was very old, and heard all that his sons did unto all Israel; and how they lay with the women that assembled at the door of the tabernacle of the congregation."

Hophni and Phinehas turned a place of holiness into a place of wickedness. They took a sacred place and turned it into a sensual place. These two young men misused their position as spiritual leaders to take advantage of women who came to worship God.

Eli loved and served the Lord, but he wasn't exempt from wrong. As a parent, he responded incorrectly to his son's wickedness. In fact, God said that he dishonored God: "Wherefore kick ye at my sacrifice and at mine offering, which I have commanded in my habitation; and honourest thy sons above me, to make yourselves fat with the chiefest of all the offerings of Israel my people?" (1 Samuel 2:29). When Eli had to make a choice between doing what was right or protecting his children, he chose his sons over God.

A leader who allows people under him to continue in wickedness brings dishonor to the name of God. Eli hated the thought of confronting his sons; he thought it would be easier to just let things slide rather than deal with the problem.

Eli didn't demand that either son change his wicked behavior or be removed from his position. He avoided his responsibility, both as their father and a leader in Israel, and God pronounced judgment on Eli for this. "For I have told him that I will judge his house for ever for the iniquity which he knoweth; because his sons made themselves vile, and he restrained them not" (1 Samuel 3:13).

Although Eli's sons were grown men and responsible for their own choices and conduct, Eli had a responsibility to confront them over their actions in this position of leadership as priests. Neither leaders nor parents will always see their followers or children do what is right. But they always have a responsibility to deal with the problem. Eli could have stopped his sons from stealing the sacrifices and committing immorality at the tabernacle by removing them from the positions they were abusing.

We cannot keep our children from ever doing wrong. Eli certainly couldn't prevent Hophni and Phinehas from sinning. Still, we must deal with the sin as it becomes known, just as Eli should have.

This behavior did not come without ramifications. What happened to Eli and his sons is a sobering reminder to us of how to respond to our own children's disobedience. First Samuel 3:11 says, "And the LORD said to Samuel, Behold, I will do a thing in Israel, at which both the ears of every one that heareth it shall tingle." Did you catch the descriptive language in this verse? The punishment God was going to bring on Eli and his family would cause people to sit up and listen until their ears "tingled."

God declared to Samuel that because of Eli's failure to deal with the sins of his sons, the entire family would be judged. "For I have told him that I will judge his house for ever for the iniquity which he knoweth; because his sons made themselves vile, and he restrained them not. And therefore I have sworn unto the house of Eli, that the iniquity of Eli's house shall not be purged with sacrifice nor offering for ever" (1 Samuel 3:13–14).

Eli's descendants would never again be trusted with the privilege and responsibility of the priesthood. It is a serious thing to fail as a leader of God's people.

James highlighted this same truth: "My brethren, be not many masters, knowing that we shall receive the greater condemnation" (James 3:1).

The judgment God pronounced did indeed come to pass. In a single day, Hophni and Phinehas were killed in battle (1 Samuel 4:11). When Eli heard the news, he fell over backward and broke his neck. Just as God had promised, the judgment was swift, sure, and final. Eli failed completely when it came to dealing with the trouble in his sons' lives.

When we see our children doing wrong, we need to confront it. Our children may not end up killed in battle, and we may not die of a broken neck, but God always deals with sins that dishonor His name.

David and His Sons—Eli wasn't the only father that failed when his sons turned their back on the Lord. King David did so as well.

David's family life was filled with drama. Repeatedly, he had to deal with problems with his sons. On three distinct occasions, we see how he dealt with his sons and what the result was in each case.

Before David died, he designated Solomon to be his heir. But that choice did not meet with unanimous approval. Adonijah was David's fourth son and older than Solomon. He decided that he should be king instead, and before David even died, he tried to set himself up on the throne.

> *Then Adonijah the son of Haggith exalted himself, saying, I will be king: and he prepared him chariots and horsemen, and fifty men to run before him. And his father had not displeased him at any time in saying, Why hast thou done so? and he also was a very goodly man; and his mother bare him after Absalom*—1 KINGS 1:5–6

Adonijah might well have become king except for the intervention of Nathan and Bathsheba with David. His effort failed, and Solomon took the throne.

But it is fascinating to see what the verses above say about David's parenting. He had never called Adonijah to account for his conduct. Basically, David let him do anything that he wanted.

We see that kind of indulgent parenting today. Experts encourage parents to never make their children unhappy. There are movements in the educational community to abolish grades. Some schools will not let the children play games in which they keep score to make sure there aren't any losers. In the end, however, this lack of boundaries will only hurt a child. Children need discipline, guidelines, and absolutes in their lives.

Because David indulged Adonijah, Adonijah became selfish. This is only natural. If you teach young children they should get everything they want, they will come to believe that they are entitled to whatever they want as they grow older. It is not uncommon for the youngest child in a family to be spoiled because he is treated differently by the parents than the older children were. While it may seem kind and loving to give your children everything they want, in the long run, it's not best for the child.

The story of Adonijah isn't the only story we find that shows David's struggles with parenting. We can also see it in the life of Absalom.

When Amnon (David's oldest son) raped his half-sister, Tamar, Absalom (Tamar's full brother), was furious. When David refused to deal with the issue, Absalom waited two years and then arranged for Amnon's murder. He then fled to his mother's homeland and stayed there for three years. Finally, David let Absalom come home, but he refused to allow him to come back to the palace.

Two more years went by without Absalom's being allowed into David's presence. Because David was indifferent to him, Absalom became seditious. Though David finally allowed Absalom to return to Jerusalem, Absalom never did fully forgive David. Their relationship was never restored.

Because of Absalom's bitterness over David's indifference, Absalom mounted a rebellion against him.

He gathered an army and tried to take over the throne. But I have to wonder: if David had been actively involved in Absalom's life when Absalom was younger, how much would the story have changed? Absalom was responsible for his actions, but David had a part in it too by being an absentee father. When we fail to raise our children to love and serve the Lord, it shouldn't come as a big surprise when they follow the rebellious path of Absalom. We have a serious responsibility to train and nurture our children in the ways of the Lord.

Although David had failed with other children, he spent the time with Solomon to give him the skills to be a good king over the people. Among other things, he instructed Solomon on the importance of wisdom, saying, "Only the Lord give thee wisdom and understanding, and give thee charge concerning Israel, that thou mayest keep the law of the Lord thy God" (1 Chronicles 22:12).

Because David instructed Solomon, Solomon became spiritual. He became a seeker after God. While Solomon did not follow the Lord for his whole life, David started him out in the right direction. There is no substitute for parental instruction. I thank God for every faithful Sunday school teacher and Christian school teacher. I thank God for every faithful youth worker and pastor. But none of them can fully play the role that God has designed for parents to fill. The primary training agency always has been and always will be the home.

The Greatest Classroom

The best classroom a child can have is in the home. Parents are meant to be the primary instructors and role models for the children. Doing so requires a huge investment of time and effort. There are no shortcuts or substitutes for extended, intensive, and personal teaching. Day after day, time after time, you must teach your children. The most important discipling you will ever do is that of your own children.

Discipline, truth, and the repetition of the Word of God have a powerful effect. Years ago, a preacher told a story about a boy working on a farm. The farmer told him to take a sieve down to the creek, fill it with water, and then bring it back. By the time the boy returned, all the water had dripped out through the holes.

The boy, somewhat discouraged, "It's empty." The farmer replied, "Yes, but now it's clean."

Like the water flowing through the sieve, you want God's Word to flow through your children. If they are taught and exposed to Scripture, that truth is in them. And according to the principle in Proverbs, they will ultimately recognize the truth of what you are teaching and follow the Lord.

As you train and admonish your children, however, there is an important truth to keep in mind. We are never to *provoke* our children to wrath.

When God gives a negative command in the Bible, it is to call our attention to something that is important to avoid. Ephesians 6:4 both warns and instructs, "And, ye fathers, provoke not your children to wrath: but bring them up in the nurture and admonition of the Lord."

How do we provoke our children to wrath? Matthew Henry says *provoking* refers to a person who, by continued haranguing, becomes to the child an enemy instead of a friend. No matter what your child does, it is never an excuse to provoke to wrath.

Not provoking your children does not mean they will never be upset with a decision you make or a discipline you enforce. When those times come, you must be sure that the discipline is given in love. If you discipline out of anger, frustration, or shame, you are not training your children, rather, you are provoking them. Angry children do not follow their parents; they rebel against them and against everything they believe.

Don't discipline your children in anger. Sometimes, you may have to wait an hour or two to get in control of your emotions (assuming they are not doing something life-threatening) so you can discipline properly. Discipline should never be done in the heat of the moment, but rather carried out in a measured, controlled, and biblical way.

I remember my father sitting down across from me when I had done something wrong. He would review the situation, making me tell him what I had done. He would ask me questions to determine that I knew why what I had done was wrong. Then he would ask me what the punishment for that offense was supposed to be. I hated that question. By disciplining in that way, he made it difficult for me to blame him for the punishment. Instead, I accepted responsibility for what I had done.

As parents, there is so much we can do to raise our children to love, serve, and honor God. From a young age, teach your children the truth. Benjamin Franklin once said, "An ounce of prevention is worth a pound of cure." It's hard (although not impossible) to help your children get victory over a temptation if they've already developed an appetite for it.

Helpful Responses to Struggle

Maybe you feel like it's too late. You can't teach your children the truth as a preventative measure because they're already turning their back on you, the Lord, and the principles you believe.

It's not too late. No matter if your child is in junior high and starting to show some teenage rebellion or if your child is older and contemplating completely leaving the faith, it's never too late for God to work in His children's lives. We saw from the lives of Eli and David that indifference to the struggles our children face is the worst response we could make. Now let's look at some positive responses.

Teach them to obey first and seek an explanation later. I often told my daughters, "First we obey, and then we explain." Children should never be given the idea that everything is subject to negotiation. Obedience protects children, and they need to learn it at an early age. It is not wrong to explain the *why* behind the *what*—in fact, it is important—but that is not the first priority.

Caution them to expect unfair treatment. Life will not be fair, and there is no reason to teach your kids to expect it to be so. Prepare them for things to go wrong and to be treated wrongly. Do not give them an expectation of entitlement. They need to know how to respond properly when they are mistreated.

Demonstrate grief for their sin rather than embarrassment for your shame. When children do something wrong, parents are often more upset for their own reputation. While children do reflect on the parents by their conduct, the reason to discipline them is to keep them from doing wrong, not to keep them from making you look bad.

Listen to their side. When your children get in trouble, ask them what happened. That does not mean that you should believe everything they say. Compare it against the evidence. As President Reagan used to say, "Trust, but verify." But do not punish a child until you know what he has to say regarding what happened.

Ask questions and avoid accusations. Sometimes children get into trouble because what they did was misunderstood. Listen carefully to what they have to say. Questions stir the conscience; accusations harden the will. God established this pattern with Adam and Eve in the Garden of Eden. He knew the answers already, thus He questioned them, not to acquire information, but to stir their consciences. (See Genesis 3:9–13.)

Support the position of authority even when you can't support the practice. Teachers, coaches, and pastors will make mistakes. When those cases happen, don't undermine their authority with your children, even if you don't agree with what they have done. Teach your children the truth that all authority is ordained by God, no matter what kind of decisions authority makes (Romans 13:1).

Several years ago, a young man from a godly family was expelled from the Christian school operated by his church. Though the father disagreed with the severity of the punishment, he said, "We are not going to leave the church. We will not attack those we feel wronged our son. We will accept this situation as from the hand of God." The young man was readmitted the following year and finished school. He went to Bible college and returned to that same church to be a successful Christian pastor. It is likely that his story would have played out differently had his parents attacked the authority that expelled him. But I believe his parents' respect for authority was a major reason why he didn't turn his back on the Lord.

Determine to grow spiritually yourself through the experience. It is difficult to see your children go through trouble, but in addition to helping them through it, look on it as an opportunity to draw closer to God yourself. As you humble yourself, you can receive God's grace in ways you need to properly guide your children (1 Peter 5:5–6).

Look for any areas that you need to strengthen. When your child gets in trouble, evaluate the example you have set for them. It may be that their problem is a result of a weakness in your life. Take the challenge to accept responsibility for areas in which you may have failed to model the right pattern of behavior. Ask the Lord for help to grow in the areas you struggle in.

Encourage your child to grow spiritually through the experience. Help them to look at their problem as an opportunity to grow closer to God. Show them God's plan for us when things go wrong and we respond properly.

Look for any areas that your child needs to strengthen. Find verses of Scripture that deal with their specific areas of weakness and have them memorize them. Use Bible examples to help them find ways they can become stronger as Christians. Make sure they understand the connection between that weakness in their character and the problem they are experiencing.

See the hand of God in the situation. Even if everyone involved in a situation is intentionally being unfair and unkind, God is still able to use that for good. Joseph suffered unjustly, but "…God meant it unto good…" (Genesis 50:20). God used the bad behavior of others to bring His purpose to fulfillment in Joseph's life.

Determine not to go backward in any area of your Christian life. Do not stop going to church, reading your Bible, or working for the Lord. Failure in one area of the Christian life does not mean you should or must fail in others. Do not allow what happens to your child to drive a wedge between you and God.

Do not try to justify yourself or your children to others. I have learned over the years that it is almost always a waste of time to try to explain what happened to people who are not involved in the situation. If you have made things right with God, stay faithful to Him. Don't allow the opinions and comments of others to steal your joy and peace.

At some point, your children will struggle—it's a natural part of life and of parenting. But when that happens, make sure your children know that it doesn't symbolize "the end." They still have a life and a future. God wants to use them and will bring good out of the struggle if we respond appropriately. Above all, make sure your children know that you love them and believe in their future.

SEVEN

PREPARING YOUR CHILDREN TO LEAVE HOME

A man had two sons, both on the brink of adulthood. This father had done his best to raise these boys to do right, but one day, the youngest son decided he wanted to leave home. He demanded that his father give him his inheritance, and the father finally agreed.

Soon after, the son packed his bags and set out to enjoy his new-found freedom. Unfortunately, he made poor choices. He lived a decadent, immoral lifestyle and soon ran out of money.

With no options, no friends, and no money, this young man took the unglamorous job of feeding pigs. Finally, he became so hungry that he actually contemplated eating what the pigs ate. At that point, he recognized that it was time for him to return to his father and beg for forgiveness. He hoped that his father would at least allow him to remain a servant in what was once the boy's family home.

The ending to this young boy's story, however, was the opposite of what he expected. His father saw him far down the road and ran to greet his long-lost son. The father immediately forgave and restored him. In fact, he even threw a celebration because he was so overjoyed at his son's return.

This is Jesus' parable of the prodigal son, found in Luke 15:11–24. It's an incredible story with God's fingerprints of mercy, forgiveness, and love all over it. It reveals that, no matter how far we wander away from our Heavenly Father, He'll always welcome us back to His table with open arms. It showcases an amazing contrast between a life lived God's way and a life devastated and degraded by sin.

I would like to look at this story from a different angle, however. Think of it with me from the perspective of a parent/child relationship, especially of a child who struggled as he left home. The indication of the story is that the prodigal son grew up in a good home, but he abandoned his beliefs when he gained independence. Likewise, many of us have seen Christian young people grow up in a good family. They never have a problem with their parents or teachers. They are pliable, compliant, and obedient. They never yell in rebellion. They never raise their hand in defiance. They never stomp out of the room in anger. But then they turn eighteen. All of a sudden, it's as if they never had any Christian training or were taught right from wrong. They throw off the restrictions and regulations they lived under, saying, "I'm free to do whatever *I* want to do."

When young people leave home, it can be a vulnerable time for them, and it is definitely a season of transition for us as parents. But as parents, it's not something we should fear—in fact, if we've been following biblical parenting principles, independence is something we've been preparing our children for their entire lives. It should be one of our greatest desires that our children live to please the Lord and impact the next generation. A pastor I knew wisely once said, "You don't know what kind of a parent you are until you see how your grandchildren turn out!"

The moment when they leave home is a culmination of eighteen years of prayer and training and is definitely a season of change for both parents and the young adult. As a parent, you want this transition to be positive and for your child to succeed through it. How do you prepare them for this?

How Much Independence and When?

The young man who became the prodigal son seemed to have had a good upbringing, but when he became an adult, he left home and made unwise choices. In this chapter, I'd like us to look at his story and for tendencies that we may detect in our own children's lives, specifically noting how we can help our children avoid the fate of the prodigal son.

To start, let's look at a few questions to ask ourselves as our children begin to desire more independence.

Is my child old enough and mature enough to be independent? As your children begin the transition into adulthood, ask yourself, "Is my child ready for this independence? What boundaries need to be in my child's life to help him stay on the right path?" One of the greatest dangers in this transitional time is allowing our children to have too much independence before they are ready.

The prodigal son wanted independence, but he didn't want it in the right way or at the right time. What he said to his father might have gone like this:

"Dad, let me leave home—give me my inheritance now."

"But son," the father might have said, "You're not ready yet. Why don't you wait a few years?"

"I don't want to wait. I think I'm ready now," the Prodigal Son may have replied.

Was it wrong for the prodigal son to want independence? No, that's a natural feeling all of us get. About junior high, most of us began wanting to pick out our own clothes and do our own hair. We told our parents, "I can do it myself." I remember asking my junior high-aged nephew if he needed help with something once. He looked at me and said, "I got it, man."

Just like my nephew, the prodigal son was convinced that "he got it." Unfortunately, he wasn't ready for his independence. His story might have turned out entirely differently had his father remained strong in telling him no.

Our children may not understand why other parents allow their children to do something that we've told them they can't do. While telling our children *no* isn't easy, it's sometimes one of the best ways we can protect them.

I believe, for example, that parents often prematurely give their children independence in dating. I've met some parents who allow their children to date at twelve years old. No matter how mature your children are, that's pretty young to begin dating, especially when you consider that they have at least six years—and likely more—until marriage. Every child is different. But I've learned, in my years of pastoring and counseling, that dating this young can present serious temptation. Couples can find it challenging to remain pure after three or more years of serious dating, especially when they know marriage is still so far away.

This mentality of "it's fine to date at any age" is common in churches, and I don't think many parents stop to consider the potential consequences. That dating culture is what I grew up in—it was normal to me. But as I grew older, I saw problems begin to arise. I started examining it in light of the Bible. Slowly, I realized that dating at such a young age isn't a biblical concept. I started teaching the young people in our church that they shouldn't date until they were older (my rule for my daughters was sixteen). Even then, I believed dating should be a double date with Mom and Dad. Because they were still young teenagers, I wanted to provide a level of accountability for them by being there.

Some people think that experience is the best teacher in dating. But I like what Henry Ford said: "The problem with the school of experience is that by the time a man graduates he is too old to work!" It is far better for children to learn from us than from experience.

Experience is a hard teacher. Although a few things are best learned by experience, we can protect our children from unnecessary consequences by slowly allowing them independence as they mature. I like to say that I've been delivered from a life of drunkenness, idolatry, addiction, and immorality. I was delivered from all those things before I ever did them, in part because of the protection and guidance of my parents. It has in no way hindered my ability to enjoy life because I have been morally pure. I am thankful for parents who helped ensure that I was ready for independence.

Can my child pay for his independence? Have you heard a question like one of these before?

"Dad, would you buy me a car so I can drive it around anywhere I want?"

"Mom, I want to be free and live on my own. By the way, here's my laundry. Could you get it done before tomorrow, please?"

"Dad, I'm old enough to go to college. I don't want to keep you updated on my grades, and I want to make my own decisions, but I'm a little short on money. Could you help me out?"

The prodigal son didn't say, "Dad, I think I'd like to go make my own way in the world. I'd like to get a job and start paying for my expenses. I'll pay for the rent on my own apartment and the insurance on my car. I'll buy my gasoline and pay for my dental insurance, my doctor's bills, and all of my food and clothing. It's time for me to stand on my own two feet." That would be responsible and an indication that he was ready for independence. Instead, he basically said, "Give me." The Bible says, "And the younger of them said to his father, Father, give me the portion of goods that falleth to me. And he divided unto them his living" (Luke 15:12). He wanted his father to pay for all of his expenses.

Instill responsibility in your children. Teach them to be wise stewards of their money. Impress on them the importance of being hard workers. Remind them not to spend something that they do not have. If your child is not willing to help work and pay for his independence, it's unlikely that he is truly ready to be independent.

Am I saying yes to this independence just to avoid more confrontation? The prodigal son's father answered his son wrongly. Instead of saying no, he gave in to his son's demands because he didn't want a confrontation.

Every child is different. Some children have no problem accepting the boundaries put on them. Others will push every limitation. Even if they know in their hearts they won't get away with disobedience, they will still try to pull off their scheme. We need to be aware of both as parents.

My daughter Katie is a born negotiator. We joke that she could mediate the problem in the Middle East. When she was young, she would tell my wife not to make a specific decision about something she wanted to do or a rule that she broke. She'd say something such as, "What if I get all my piano practice done, all my homework done, and get my room cleaned up? What if I do this, and what if I do that?" Katie isn't a rebel, but she still tried to test the rules. Your children may not throw an outright temper tantrum when they do not get their way, but they may question the rules you set in place.

Stomping out of rooms, slammed doors, raised voices, and rolled eyes quickly grow tiring. Those behaviors are not appropriate and should not be allowed. But too often, parents will give in to the forceful demands of their child.

That's what happened to the prodigal son. The Bible says the father, "divided unto them his living" (Luke 15:12). After demanding his share of money, the prodigal son left home and prepared to set out on his own.

You may have a child on the verge of becoming another prodigal son. You're tired of the confrontation and tension in the home. My encouragement to you is to keep being a godly, strong parent even when it's difficult. Do all that you can to prevent your child from making wrong decisions that lead him down the path of the prodigal son.

Does my child understand the biblical principles behind my rules and standards? The Bible doesn't say much about the prodigal son's home life, but I think we can assume that he was a "church kid" that knew what was right. Still, when he left home, he was basically saying, "My dad believes this way, but I don't. I will not be like my parents were." We see this further in the description of how he lived: "And not many days after the younger son gathered all together, and took his journey into a far country, and there wasted his substance with riotous living" (Luke 15:13).

You cannot expect your children to do something or believe something just because you do. As they grow older, their actions and beliefs must come from a heart anchored to the truths of the Bible.

I remember the story Dr. John R. Rice told of his daughter. She was engaged to marry what seemed to be a wonderful man. They'd sent out wedding invitations, been given a bridal shower, and were looking forward to the wedding just a short time away. But the man told her, "I can't wait until I can get you out from all these rules and regulations here. You won't have to live by your daddy's standards anymore."

Dr. Rice's daughter looked at that young man and said, "My daddy's standards are my standards. My daddy's beliefs are my beliefs." Immediately, she called off the wedding and sent the gifts back.

Unfortunately, more people are like the prodigal son than they are like Dr. Rice's daughter. When young people who grow up in Christian homes suddenly depart from what they've been taught, it is because their parent's standards never became a heart belief for them.

The prodigal son threw off all that he had been taught in order to do what he wanted to do. It's likely that he complied with the list of rules his father had given him while he was at home, but he never understood the principles behind those rules.

Although we can never *make* our children do right, we can *teach* them what is right and wrong and the biblical principle behind it. If our children only look at rules as a list of do's and don'ts but don't have an appreciation and understanding of biblical principles behind them, one day they will be faced with a new temptation that isn't on their list of rules. If they don't understand biblical principles behind the rules we set for them, it will be easy for them to succumb to a temptation not on their list.

One example of how rules and principles should be connected can be seen in how Christians look at the movie industry. For instance, there are Christians who have a personal standard to never attend a movie theater. But some of the same Christians who would never enter a theater will watch blatant immorality on their televisions or phone screens. They have a standard (to not to go to the movie theater), but they never grasped the biblical principle behind it (to set no wicked thing before their eyes, from Psalm 101:3). When children live their entire life under standards without understanding the biblical reasons behind them, it's easy for them to shrug off what they've learned and do what they feel is right. Your message to your children is more credible when you can show them the biblical reason behind why you do what you do.

I want my children to keep the standards I've taught them, but even more importantly, I want them to have biblical principles. Even if they interpret standards differently, they'll be biblically grounded.

In other words, I want my children to be Bereans. The Bible describes the Bereans in Acts 17:11: "These were more noble than those in Thessalonica, in that they received the word with all readiness of mind, and searched the scriptures daily, whether those things were so." The Bereans in this passage weighed what was said against the

Scripture. Because truth must come from the Bible, they were protected from the errors of thinking that often creep into lives and churches.

I've told our congregation, "If you think that you can follow me just because you like me, someday you may follow me into error. But if you follow me as I follow Christ (1 Corinthians 11:1), you'll recognize if something I say is wrong and correct it." I do my best to teach what Scripture says, but I want people to measure what I say against the Bible.

We need to teach our children the Word of God. If there is one class in our Christian school that I want our children to grow, learn, and memorize in, if there's one class that I think really is worthy of a large share of a child's time, it is Bible class. I want my children to know the truth.

As your children grow older and become adults, they may not agree with the application of a principle or the standard you've established. But if you've taught them biblical principles, it is more likely that they will still follow the Word of God, even after they've left the home.

When the Prodigal Son ran into trouble, he didn't go home immediately. Instead, he took a job feeding pigs. Remember, these were unclean animals for the Jews. There could be no more degrading a responsibility, no more unpleasant a task, than feeding the pigs for this young man. But this man was so desperate for help that he actually began coveting the pigs' food (Luke 15:16).

Many times, parents assume that when things get a little tough, their child will come back. This is true in some cases, but often a wayward child won't return home before they spend some time in the pigpen. Parents, it's so important that we give our children a *why* behind the *what*. But most importantly, we need to give them the *who* behind the *what*. Behind every policy, there ought to be a principle. Behind every principle, there ought to be a person we're trying to please—the Lord Jesus Christ. As your children prepare to leave home, ask yourself if they are ready. If your children haven't reached that stage yet, continue with the Holy Spirit's help to help them live a God-pleasing and God-honoring life before they leave your home.

Roots of Rebellion

Parents who have watched their children turn their back on the Lord have questions. They want to know why their child simply abandoned what they had been taught. To answer these questions requires understanding the heart of the matter. When we see the root of a young adult's rebellion, it's easier to understand and help a young adult repent and come back to the Lord, as the prodigal son did.

In the Old Testament, we get a convicting glimpse into what happens when a spiritual leader is no longer in a person's life (such as when a child leaves a godly home). Joshua led the Israelites across the Jordan River and into the Promised Land. After they conquered the Canaanites, he divided that land and gave them their inheritance. When Joshua died, the children of Israel kept serving God—for a while. The Bible says that they served God all the days of Joshua and all the days of the elders who outlived Joshua, who had seen the works that God had done. But when that generation was gone, the people turned away from God (Judges 2:11-13). Why did they do this? Why wasn't the faith of their fathers real to them?

It's difficult to watch a child you loved and raised suddenly turn his back on his upbringing. Every child is ultimately responsible for his decision. But as we look at rebellion, we can detect some common roots:

A wrong purpose—When I ask young people, "Why do you want to leave home?" I have never yet had someone reply, "I desire to be a drunkard. I want to be a drug addict. I want to make my life a mess and get all kinds of diseases. I want to have children out of wedlock. I want to get married and have it end in terrible tragedy and divorce. That's my goal for my life."

Why, then, has that happened time and time again? Often, young people get in trouble because they have the wrong purpose.

No one likes being told what to do. No matter how submissive we are, there will always be a built-in human tendency to resist authority. Just think about what happens when we see a sign that says "Wet Paint." Immediately, we want to reach out to see if it's wet.

It's not wrong for young people to look forward to being an adult and making their own decisions. In fact, your children should be motivated to leave home to chase whatever God has for their lives.

The problem arises when the motive for leaving is a dislike of being under the authority of another and desire to lead their own lives without any instruction. These young people simply want to follow their flesh.

As parents, we should establish boundaries to help protect our children from sinning. Sometimes, however, young people rub against these boundaries and want to go their own way. To them, being independent seems to be the best way to accomplish this. The devil wants to give people opportunities to satisfy the desires of the flesh. He is a master at offering the perfect chance to do wrong. When the Prodigal Son got to the far country, he didn't have to look hard to find places to waste his substance. He found the opportunities to sin that he left home to find. Ultimately, however, he ended up in a pigpen.

An inaccurate view of life—Maybe you've heard about the young man who said, "I am fed up with being told what to do. I'm tired of my mother. She tells me when to get up, how to dress, and when to go to bed. She's always fussing at me about my posture. I am going to run away and join the Marines!" That young man had a wrong perspective of life.

I experienced that firsthand. The extent of my teenage rebellion was leaving home at fifteen to join an academy that was part of a Bible college. I remember being so eager to get there. I looked forward to my mother not telling me when to get up or go to bed, how to clean my room, how to dress, or how much homework I still had to do. I couldn't wait to get out from under all the rules and restrictions I had at home.

I was in for a reality check. When I arrived, I stayed in the same dorms as the college students. I was treated like them too. For example, I was required to get up every morning at 6:55 and go to bed every night at 11:00. Every day I had to clean the sink and the mirror, dust the furniture, and mop the floor or empty the trash. In fact, I was even required to make my bed.

At this academy, you had to make a B average or attend study hall and sit in a classroom from 7:00–9:30 four nights a week. After weeks of hard work, I got that B average and avoided study hall. But during the next grading period, I went to the gym or the pool and fooled around every night when I should have been studying. It was no surprise that by the next grading period, I ended up right back in study hall because I did not maintain my B average.

There will always be someone with the authority to tell us what to do. Think about the President and the restrictions on his life. He can't get out and go to the grocery store. He has far less control over his schedule than we do. He can't walk down a public street. He can't go to a mall. If he wants to go someplace on vacation, it takes dozens of Secret Service people days to prepare to block everything off and keep him safe.

No one is absolutely free. Everyone has someone telling him what to do in at least some part of his life. The Prodigal Son thought, *I'm tired of my father's house. I'm tired of the restrictions. I'm tired of the rules, regulations, and requirements. I want out of here!* He thought living in freedom would be better than living in his father's house.

But the prodigal son was wrong. The worst day in his father's house was better than his best day in the pigpen. When he was under the rule of his father, he was better off than wasting all of his money on his own. What he thought would be a fun time of freedom turned into a horrific time compared to the years he spent in his father's house. This letdown he inevitably experienced could be, in part, attributed to a wrong perspective of life.

Most young people believe that everything will turn out well. They have a hard time considering the consequences and understanding the long-term results of their behavior. This isn't even a bad thing—when we're young, we don't like to think about when we will be older.

Perhaps you've heard of Mickey Mantle, the outstanding baseball player. He died of liver failure and complications brought on by years of drinking. Before he died, he said, "If I had known I was going to live this long, I would have taken better care of myself!" By then, it was too late.

As parents, we need to be teaching our children what it's like being an adult. It is a wonderful time of independence, but along with it comes responsibility. Young people who believe independence will solve all of their problems carry an inaccurate view of life. Furthermore, they are likely to quickly run into trouble because they haven't learned responsibility.

Lack of preparation for the future—Parents often have a hand in this—we don't want our children to grow up, so we may fail to prepare them. I remember asking my girls when they were very young, "Are you going to grow up?" They solemnly promised they wouldn't. Later, I found out they lied to me! One day, our children will become adults. We need to prepare them to leave home and be independent of us.

I've seen in the lives of some parents something psychologists call *codependency*. Basically, this is the idea that in a relationship, two people can become too dependent on the other person.

Sometimes, we can see this in a counselor/counselee relationship. The counselor needs to be needed by the counselee, and the counselee needs someone to give him a sense of security and tell him what to do. The counselor needs his ego affirmed by someone wanting his advice, and the counselee needs his insecurity addressed by someone giving him direction for life. Instead of truly helping each other, they are locked into a never-ending relationship.

As a parent, avoid creating an unhealthy level of dependence with your child. You want your children to have the right foundation to make good choices when they've left the home.

Parenting extends far beyond just providing food and shelter. It also includes preparing our children for the future.

For example, we need to teach our children about money. If your children are young, give them a small amount of money and watch how they spend it. Tell them to try to make it last for a certain period of time. Let them plan for upcoming youth activities and school lunches with the money you've given them, and see if there's any money left at the end. Teach them the expression "having too much month left at the end of the money," and show them how to keep that from happening.

Teach your children how to cook. Show them how to change the oil, do some basic repairs on a lawn mower, or put a washer on a faucet.

Help your children prepare for independence by showing them how to respond when temptation arises.

When our daughters were little, we would ask, "If a boy ever wanted to date you, what would you say?" They would reply, "Ask Mom and Dad." We would continue, "What if we say no?" The right answer was, "I wouldn't date him." Karissa would usually add, "I'd find someone else!" Then we'd say, "Where would be a really fun place to go on a date?" They would say, "Home to play board games with Mom and Dad and the boy."

Then we would ask, "Would you ever date a boy who wasn't saved? Would you ever date a boy who wasn't a committed Christian?" They would say, "No." I started doing that when they were three and four. Of course, I didn't expect my children to begin dating for several more years. But when that day came, I wanted them to be ready.

You want to do everything you can to spiritually and practically prepare your children for adulthood.

Rebellion isn't something that just happens one morning. A child or teen doesn't wake up and think, "I guess it's time to start being rebellious." It's a process that has definite roots. If we're aware of those roots, we can prepare our children to avoid the pull of rebellion and smoothly transition into adult independence.

Practical Steps to Preparing Our Children for Independence

No matter where you are on your parenting journey, it's not too late to prepare your children for independence. This begins with training our children.

It appears that the Prodigal Son's father did not do well in this area. Even a brief look at our story reveals that this young man either had no idea how to handle money or completely rejected his father's teaching. He didn't know how to take an investment and make something out of it. As a result, he was not prepared to live on his own. It's not enough just to tell your children the truth—you need to train them effectively so that they will do what is right.

Additionally, we must teach our children to listen and obey the first time we ask them to do something. Don't be discouraged when it seems like your children are not getting it, especially in the early years of parenting. You may have to repeat this concept to your children before they finally listen. Don't feel like a failure if this happens to you—training is never a waste of time. Even if it seems that you're making no progress, there is work being done on the inside of which neither the person doing the training nor the person being worked on is fully aware.

One day, even years down the road, children will remember what they have been taught if you are diligent to teach them the truth when they are young.

When God offered Solomon anything that he desired, Solomon could have made many different choices. Think about it—he could have asked for riches, power, or long life. I think many of us would be tempted to do that. Instead, however, he chose a wise heart. When Solomon was young, David had taught him the importance of wisdom. Then, when Solomon was confronted with one of the biggest decisions of his life, he chose wisely.

> *For I was my father's son, tender and only beloved in the sight of my mother. He taught me also, and said unto me, Let thine heart retain my words: keep my commandments, and live. Get wisdom, get understanding: forget it not; neither decline from the words of my mouth. Forsake her not, and she shall preserve thee: love her, and she shall keep thee.* **Wisdom is the principal thing; therefore get wisdom:** *and with all thy getting get understanding.*
> —PROVERBS 4:3–7

Finally, we need to let our children make mistakes. It's an obvious statement—children independent of Mom and Dad don't have Mom and Dad to guide them. By letting our children fail, we're preparing them for life as independent adults. Don't let your children have the option of sinning, but do let them make a decision between a better choice and a lesser choice.

For example, I would not let my child choose between going to church and staying home to watch television. I would, on the other hand, let them choose between doing their homework the night before a test and playing video games. As a parent, you might say something like this, "You know you have a test tomorrow, and you told me you hadn't studied very much, but if you want to, go ahead and play the game. I think you ought to study, but you can make your own choice." Then, when they flunk and they're off the ball team or have to repeat a class, they'll have learned from that mistake.

You're not a poor parent if you allow your child to make some mistakes. Protect them from harmful or sinful mistakes, but let them see the consequences of their bad behavior.

The Importance of Independence

It is dangerous to give children independence too early. But it is also dangerous to give children independence too late. If you never let your children make a decision, it will be difficult for them to know how to choose. You must prepare your children now, because sooner than you think they will leave home. Make sure they are ready before they leave.

Watching your children leave home should be a bittersweet moment. It's bitter because it's never easy for parents to say goodbye to their child. It's sweet because, if you've trained your children correctly, you'll be able to watch them continue serving the Lord joyfully.

Is parenting difficult? Yes, definitely. But is it worth it? Absolutely. There is nothing more joyful than watching your children grow up to serve the Lord. And you, as their parent, have the opportunity to mentor them into becoming what God has created them to be.

EIGHT

UNDERSTANDING DIVORCE

I've been a pastor for decades. I've seen people walk through unimaginably difficult times. The stories of these people make my heart hurt for them. Divorce is one of those unimaginably difficult times. No matter the circumstances, it's a time of intense pressure. And while I never suggest or advocate divorce to a couple, I do recognize how deeply and brutally it impacts so many lives.

We live in a love-crazed world. Everywhere we turn, it seems that there is a new book, TV show, or magazine article promising the secret to a successful marriage. Dating websites are widely accepted. Flip through the guide on your television, and you'll likely see a talk show on how to create a healthy marriage or a new movie advertised about falling in love. Love and marriage are heavily emphasized in our world.

Why, then, is divorce so common? Some researchers suggest that nearly one in two marriages end in divorce. Second, third, and fourth marriages are common. And that's not limited to the world. Unfortunately, even Christians get divorced at alarming numbers.

God places a high priority on the sanctity of marriage, and He despises divorce. In fact, God says in Malachi 2 that He hates "putting away."

> *And this have ye done again, covering the altar of the LORD with tears, with weeping, and with crying out, insomuch that he regardeth not the offering any more, or receiveth it with good will at your hand. Yet ye say, Wherefore? Because the LORD hath been witness between thee and the wife of thy youth, against whom thou hast dealt treacherously: yet is she thy companion, and the wife of thy covenant. And did not he make one? Yet had he the residue of the spirit. And wherefore one? That he might seek a godly seed. Therefore take heed to your spirit, and let none deal treacherously against the wife of his youth. For the LORD, the God of Israel, saith that he hateth*

> *putting away: for one covereth violence with his garment, saith the* LORD *of hosts: therefore take heed to your spirit, that ye deal not treacherously.*—MALACHI 2:13–16

Divorce separates what God has joined together in the marriage relationship. Jesus said in Matthew 19:8, "From the beginning it was not so." God's plan from the beginning was an "until-death-do-us-part" marriage. But while God hates divorce, it's not the unpardonable sin. God forgives and restores.

Perhaps you're reading this and you can relate all too well to the pain of divorce. You're asking yourself, *How do I move on from this? How do I get over my past? How do I forgive my spouse? How do I even forgive myself?*

Maybe, on the other hand, you haven't personally dealt with divorce, but you wonder what God has to say about it. Is it ever acceptable? How do you help a friend or a loved one who has experienced divorce? What is the role of a divorced person in the church?

In this chapter, we'll discuss a biblical view of divorce. But I want you to come at the next few pages with this viewpoint—God doesn't want any of His children to live in the past. Divorce is an unfortunate reality in our world, and it's certainly a pressure period in life. No matter what you've done, however, God wants you to live a joy-filled life of abundance in Him. And with His help, you can.

Views on Divorce

Divorce is not a simple issue. It goes much deeper than two partners going their separate ways, and anyone who has been divorced knows that. While most Christians would agree that divorce is wrong, or at least not preferred, they disagree about how Scripture interprets divorce. In Christian circles, you will find four broad approaches to divorce. Good Christians disagree on these positions. I'm sure in what I believe about divorce, and it's important that you too arrive at a position supported by Scripture.

Position 1: Divorce is never acceptable. The people who hold this view cite Luke 16:18 which says, "Whosoever putteth away his wife, and marrieth another, committeth adultery: and whosoever marrieth her that is put away from her husband committeth adultery." Christians who take this position believe that divorce for any reason is sin, that divorce is not recognized by God, and therefore that remarriage is adultery.

Position 2: Divorce is acceptable for many causes, and remarriage is permitted. Other Christians take a practically opposite view and believe divorce is acceptable if the marriage was not "in the Lord." Those with this view cite 1 Corinthians 7:39, which states, "The wife is bound by the law as long as her husband liveth; but if her husband be dead, she is at liberty to be married to whom she will; only in the Lord." I believe that this a misinterpretation of what the verse is saying, which is that Christians should only marry Christians. It does not mean get divorced if one does marry an unbeliever.

Some take this second position even further. They believe divorce is acceptable for things such as incompatibility or desertion. These are painful situations. They require an incredible amount of grace and often the help of biblical counsel to get through. I believe in these situations, however, that God gives grace to stay married, even when it's painful and difficult.

Those who add to the Bible's reasons for divorce are generally arguing (although they may not recognize it or say it this way) for divorce for any reason at all. By taking this position, it's easy to expand the Bible beyond what it says to get a desired result.

Position 3: Divorce is acceptable for fornication, but there are no grounds for remarriage. This view comes from Matthew 19:9 where Jesus said, "And I say unto you, Whosoever shall put away his wife, except it be for fornication, and shall marry another, committeth adultery: and whoso marrieth her which is put away doth commit adultery." This passage was actually a dialogue between the Pharisees and Jesus. They were questioning Him about an Old Testament law (Deuteronomy 24:1) that permitted a husband to divorce his wife.

The Pharisees questioned Jesus about this practice, looking as they often did for an opportunity to trap Him. Jesus responded by citing the original design God had for marriage. Marriage is God's ideal, and He did not mean for it to be divided by anyone. Moses made an allowance for divorce because the people had hard and stubborn hearts. However, that was not part of God's original plan.

This passage is the most extensive teaching Jesus gave on the subject of divorce. Some people read what Jesus said in this passage and conclude that, while divorce is acceptable in this one case, there is no provision for the divorced person to remarry.

Position 4: Divorce is acceptable on grounds of fornication, and, in that case, remarriage is acceptable as well. While I realize many good Christians disagree, this is the position I take. God never prefers divorce, and His will is for the partners to be reconciled and restored.

I firmly believe that God wants restoration in marriage, even after something as painful as adultery. I would never recommend divorce to someone, even after adultery. Instead, I would counsel both spouses to ask God for a miracle of restoration. (A godly Christian friend of mine told me he would not remarry a divorced person if they had a living, un-remarried spouse because he did not want to close the door on a possible reconciliation.) At the same time, I believe that, based on Matthew 19, fornication provides an exception to the unbreakable nature of marriage. Thus it is acceptable, although not required or preferred, to divorce because of fornication; and, in such a case, it is also acceptable to remarry.

Understanding this teaching of Jesus requires that we understand what He was talking about when He referred to *fornication*.

Some people teach that fornication refers only to unfaithfulness during the betrothal period. In Jewish culture, the man and woman were espoused (like Joseph and Mary), sometimes for a lengthy period, before the wedding. They were promised to each other. Some believe that fornication is limited to breaking that betrothal. But I believe this position isn't supported by Scripture.

The word translated "fornication" is the Greek word *pornea*, from which we get the word *pornography*. It is used throughout the Bible, and refers to much more than unfaithfulness during the betrothal period. There are some places where it does simply refer to the betrothal period, but more often it is clearly referring to broader contexts.

For example, when the Jerusalem Council met to consider what instructions to give the Gentile Christians, they wrote, "That ye abstain from meats offered to idols, and from blood, and from things strangled, and from *fornication*: from which if ye keep yourselves, ye shall do well. Fare ye well" (Acts 15:29). Obviously, they were not instructing new Christians to be morally pure only during their betrothals.

Fornication is a broad term that refers to various kinds of sexual impurity. *Adultery* is a subset of fornication and generally refers to immorality between married people.

Therefore, I believe that when Jesus allowed divorce in the case of fornication, He was referring to a spouse's unfaithfulness after marriage.

Furthermore, adultery is a sin with special consequences. Proverbs 6:32–33 says, "But whoso committeth adultery with a woman lacketh understanding: he that doeth it destroyeth his own soul. A wound and dishonour shall he get; and his reproach shall not be wiped away." While adultery is not a more heinous sin than others, its destructive effects are greater and longer lasting.

Adding to this, in the Old Testament, the penalty for adultery was death. Remember when the Pharisees brought the woman taken in adultery to Jesus in John 8? They were tempting Him to see if He would enforce the letter of the law. The penalty was death by stoning, but the stoning was to be carried out by the witnesses. Thus Jesus said for those who were innocent to cast the first stones at her.

With this in mind, in the Old Testament, the innocent spouse whose partner committed adultery was always able to remarry because the guilty party was dead. In the New Testament era, while we do not live under the Old Testament Jewish laws, I believe that we should extend that same opportunity to remarry that the innocent spouse had under the law. When a marriage is dissolved because of divorce over adultery, I believe the innocent party should be free to remarry.

Adultery breaks the one-flesh relationship, the very essence of marriage. Jesus said, "And said, For this cause shall a man leave father and mother, and shall cleave to his wife: and they twain shall be one flesh? Wherefore they are no more twain, but one flesh. What therefore God hath joined together, let not man put asunder" (Matthew 19:5–6). Adultery undermines the heart of the marriage relationship.

When considering this position, remember that refusing to allow biblically divorced people to remarry creates a church discipline issue. If people who are divorced and get remarried are committing adultery, it would be wrong to allow anyone who is remarried to hold any position in the church or even to be a church member. Based on that philosophy, they would be living in sin and would be subject to church discipline. Most who hold the position that remarriage is wrong would still allow remarried people to keep coming to church. I believe that is an inconsistent standard.

Another example of God permitting divorce is when He divorced Israel because of the nation's immorality. Jeremiah 3:8 says, "And I saw, when for all the causes whereby backsliding Israel committed adultery I had put her away, and given her a bill of divorce; yet her treacherous sister Judah feared not, but went and played the harlot also." For hundreds of years, God sent prophets and judges to call the people back to Himself. They refused again and again until God divorced her. Christians would disagree on this passage and its application to marriage. That being said, I believe saying that God never recognizes a divorce for any reason is saying God violates what the Bible teaches.

Ultimately, I would encourage you to be careful to form your convictions regarding divorce based on what the Bible says, not what society or even other Christians think. One fact remains, however, and that is that neither divorce nor adultery are God's plan for marriage. While God always offers grace, that does not negate the inevitable pain and suffering. How do we respond, then, to the hurt divorce causes? What should our perspective be when we're confronted with divorce?

When You Are Faced with Divorce

When you are faced with divorce, whether through your choice or your spouse's choice, what should you do? With so many unscriptural philosophies on marriage, from both the world and Christians, it can be easy not to recognize what the Bible says on the matter.

Recognize that while divorce is permitted, it is not preferred. I can't begin to imagine the pain a spouse that has been betrayed by adultery feels. The confusion, anger, and hurt that result are inevitable. But I want to challenge you to consider who our God is. He is a God of restoration. While He does allow for divorce to occur because of adultery, divorce is never His plan. I believe that, with the Lord's strength and grace, your first reaction to adultery doesn't have to be, "I'm getting a divorce." I believe that God can work a miracle of restoration, even in the most difficult circumstances.

I recognize that all situations are different, and this is not intended to be condemning, but I do believe that God gets more glory from reconciliation and rebuilding than from divorce and dissolution.

Maybe you haven't experienced adultery in your marriage. But the spark that was so strong when you first met your spouse has died out. You don't feel that connection anymore. Or maybe you argue all the time. You feel that the atmosphere in your home is tense and angry, not peaceful and happy. You and your spouse are pushing each other away, and, in your quieter moments, divorce has crossed your mind—or you've threatened your spouse outright with it in the middle of one of your arguments. When those tough times come, ask the Lord to help you restore your marriage relationship. When a couple with great problems works to rebuild a strong relationship, it is a powerful testimony to the power of God, and it brings Him glory.

Do not be the one to end the marriage or the one to end the possibility of reconciliation. I've had many couples come to my office seriously contemplating divorce, and some ultimately do divorce. But no matter the reason they give me for getting a divorce, I've never counseled them to proceed. I've encouraged them to wait and ask God to work in their lives.

If it looks like your marriage is going to be permanently broken, let it be the other person who does it rather than you. In our society, divorce is usually not avoidable if one person insists on going through with it. Still, you don't have to be the one to end the marriage. It may be that God will perform a miracle in your relationship, and you don't want to close the door on that possibility.

If you have sinned by getting an unscriptural divorce, ask the Lord to help you make things right. First, confess your sin to the Lord; then accept God's forgiveness. Don't let the devil make you feel like a second-class citizen for the rest of your life. That guilt is not from God. Your sin is in the past, just as the sins of others are in their past. Divorce doesn't prevent you from serving in the church. (The only positions divorce disqualifies someone from is that of a pastor and a deacon—see 1 Timothy 3:2, 12.) God wants to use you, and He still has an incredible plan for your life. Remember, every member of your church is a forgiven sinner. The ground is always level at the cross.

If you've been through divorce, I'd encourage you to use your experience to minister to others. Ask the Lord to give you opportunities and the courage to share the pain and suffering of divorce. You may be uniquely positioned to help someone else avoid the mistakes and heartache you have experienced.

When Others Go through a Divorce

What if someone you know and love is walking through a divorce, and you want to help them, but you're not sure how?

Understand that there are innocent parties. The most innocent parties in divorce are the children. Almost without exception, children feel responsible when their parents separate. They have a natural inclination to blame themselves and feel rejected. One of the best things that you can do is to reach out to them with acceptance and love.

There are also innocent spouses. Usually both parties in a broken marriage are at fault (no spouse is perfect), although one spouse may be more at fault than another. There are cases, however, when one spouse does nothing to end the marriage, yet the other spouse walks away.

We had a lady in our church years ago who married a young man from her Bible college. Although she did not know it, he was a homosexual. Their marriage ended, but she was not responsible for his sin or for the destruction of their marriage. Through no fault of her own, she walked through a horrible tragedy. We must be careful not to judge those who have been through a divorce—rarely do we have all the facts. Even when we do, we can recognize that what someone did was wrong, just as we would recognize any sin was wrong. But don't let your knowledge of someone's past taint your view or treatment of that person.

Respect the fact that people who have been forgiven for an unscriptural divorce are just as forgiven as those who have committed any other sin. Divorce has horrific consequences for families and for our society, and God is against it. Never forget, however, that while God hates divorce, He doesn't hate divorced people. As we strive to be more like Christ, that should be our attitude as well. We are to love, help, and encourage those who have been divorced and look for opportunities to help them. I'm thankful that God is in the forgiveness and reconciliation business. All of us have sins in our past that we are not proud of, and divorce is no different. When God forgives someone, they are completely forgiven. It is not our job, then, to subconsciously punish them by holding their past against them. And just as we mentioned before, all divorce situations are different. You may come in contact with an innocent spouse that needs your love and acceptance, not condemnation.

Many people were divorced before they got saved. Many others have a divorce in their past but have sought forgiveness for their part in it and are striving to do the best they can going forward. We should not hold people accountable for what has already been forgiven. Everyone who comes into the church starts from where they are.

If you've walked the ugly road of divorce, recognize that God freely extends His grace and, where needed, forgiveness. Once you've accepted His forgiveness, you can move on. You can experience greater moments of victory in your Christian life than you thought possible. You can live a fulfilling, joy-filled life serving the Saviour. You can truly say that the best is yet to come.

Divorce is a period of intense pressure for those who are involved—directly and indirectly. Unfortunately, it's all too common, even among Christians. It's not an easy thing. It tears apart families. It's painful. But because of God's grace, forgiveness, and love, it is also redeemable.

PART THREE

FINANCIAL PRESSURES

NINE

LOOKING AT MONEY GOD'S WAY

Fill in the blank. A godly Christian will _____. There are several words you could have put there. Maybe you thought one of these: share the gospel, attend church, read the Bible, pray.

But just as much as a godly Christian will do those things, a godly Christian will steward his money wisely. At the end of our lives, how much money we made (or didn't make) doesn't matter. Jesus warned, "...Take heed, and beware of covetousness: for a man's life consisteth not in the abundance of the things which he possesseth" (Luke 12:15). Money is a tool, not something we are to build our lives on or find our worth in.

Yet many in our world do look at money as a status symbol. Maybe you've seen the bumper sticker that says, "He who dies with the most toys wins." Biblically, that couldn't be further from the truth. God has given us money to use for Him and His glory.

Managing finances is a struggle for many Christians. Less than 30 percent of the families in America use a monthly budget to manage their money. The average American spends $1.22 for every $1.00 he earns. The personal savings rate in 2000 was 5.7 percent, and by 2006, that had fallen to 3.6 percent.

Aside from their mortgage, the typical family in America has a debt of $38,000. Ninety-five percent of the cars sold in this country are financed, and the average car payment is $375 per month. Household debt as a percentage of disposable income exceeds 100 percent—most people owe more than they are worth. People simply are not wise in the way they handle money.

And the answer to our money problems isn't just to make more money, get someone to leave an inheritance, make savvy investments, or come into an unexpected windfall. Just ask William Post. In 1988, he won $16 million in the Pennsylvania lottery. He said, "Everybody dreams of winning money, but nobody realizes the nightmares that come out of the woodwork, or the problems."

A former girlfriend sued William for part of his money. His own brother hired a hit man to kill him so he could inherit the wealth. Other siblings hounded him to invest in their businesses. He spent time in jail for shooting at a bill collector. Within a year of winning the jackpot, he was a million dollars in debt, and he eventually declared bankruptcy.[1]

If the secret to successful money managing isn't just to make more than you need or come into an unexpected windfall, what is it?

There are so many conflicting philosophies over how we're to use money.

"Definitely do this," one person says.

"Don't do that," another person contradicts.

"The secret to wealth is…" someone else promises.

"Do this with your money, and you'll be happy," another person proclaims.

It's enough to make us throw our hands up in confusion. Is there really a clear-cut answer to all of these money questions? Does God give us financial principles to follow? Does He even care how we handle our money?

The Lord does, and He gives clear direction in the Bible, not only in answering these questions, but in how to glorify Him in the use of our money.

Christians don't have an excuse for poor financial habits. Money is one of the many resources God gives us to

---

[1] Patricia Sullivan, "William 'Bud' Post III; Unhappy Lottery Winner," *Washingtonpost.com*, January 20, 2006, http://www.washingtonpost.com/wp-dyn/content/article/2006/01/19/AR2006011903124.html (accessed June 10. 2018).

manage on His behalf, and we have a responsibility to Him. Help comes as we understand what God's view of money is and then implement that in our lives.

As we explore finances in the next few chapters, my goal isn't to help you "get rich quick." Instead, I want to guide you toward biblical principles of stewardship. I want you to avoid many of the avoidable pressures that can come with poor financial planning and to overcome those you may already be experiencing.

Money itself does not make people happy, successful, stable, or secure. Only Christ can bring fulfillment into our lives. And when it comes to money, God's Word *does* teach us how to manage it wisely.

The Provision of God

The starting place for managing our money wisely is to recognize that everything we have was provided by God.

Over the years, people have said to me, "Everything I have, I got with these two hands."

But then I ask, "Where did you get your hands?"

The right attitude toward money starts with understanding biblical principles about it. Once we have that established, we can see our responsibilities toward God with our money. If our thinking in these areas is correct, we've taken the first step on wise money management. Let's look at three foundational principles about money.

God is the owner. I call this the principle of stewardship. God owns everything, but He wants us to manage—or steward—that money during our lives for Him. This principle of stewardship is so foundational that if we do not understand it, we will struggle with money our entire lives.

God tells us, "Every good gift and every perfect gift is from above, and cometh down from the Father of lights, with whom is no variableness, neither shadow of turning" (James 1:17). In Haggai 2:8, God says, "The silver is mine, and the gold is mine, saith the LORD of hosts."

Notice, God doesn't say, "Some of the silver is mind, and most of the gold is mine..." James doesn't tell us, "Almost all good gifts (except the ones you work for yourself) and most perfect gifts are from above..." Everything belongs to God.

God gives the opportunities. Deuteronomy 8:18 states, "But thou shalt remember the LORD thy God: for it is he that giveth thee power to get wealth, that he may establish his covenant which he sware unto thy fathers, as it is this day." Wealth is a blessing from the Lord. Proverbs 10:22 says, "The blessing of the LORD, it maketh rich, and he addeth no sorrow with it." This helps us understand the stewardship principle. Because God is the one who even allows us to accumulate money, we have an obligation to use it the way He wants us to.

God sets the obligation. The first obligation God sets for our money is to tithe and give. Leviticus 27:30 says, "And all the tithe of the land, whether of the seed of the land, or of the fruit of the tree, is the LORD's: it is holy unto the LORD." And Malachi 3:10 says, "Bring ye all the tithes into the storehouse, that there may be meat in mine house, and prove me now herewith, saith the LORD of hosts, if I will not open you the windows of heaven, and pour you out a blessing, that there shall not be room enough to receive it."

God owns everything, God gives us the opportunity to gain money, and God wants us to give back what He has given us.

But that leads us to pause and ask, "Why does God want my money? After all, doesn't He own the cattle on a thousands hills? Why does He want what I have? He doesn't need it to accomplish His will."

That's a valid question. If God is not limited by how much we give (or don't give), why is He so concerned about our money?

The Purpose of Money

Money is a medium of exchange. If you look at a one-dollar-bill, the value of the paper and ink is worth about five cents. But if you take it to the bank, they will give you a hundred pennies for it. That is because our nation has an economic system that has assigned a face value to various pieces of currency. Whatever the bill says on the front, we say it is worth that much money.

In America, our paper money used to be backed by gold. During the Great Depression, however, the government switched to silver. On each silver certificate (a one-dollar bill) printed between 1934 and 1963 was the statement, "This certifies that there has been deposited in the Treasury of the United States of America one silver dollar payable to the bearer on demand." If you lived during that time, you could literally take your dollar bill and trade it in for one dollar's worth of silver bullion, just as before 1934 you could take a dollar bill in and exchange it for gold.

In 1971, America abandoned this standard. Now your dollar bill says: "This note is legal tender for all debts, public and private." You can no longer trade your dollar in for silver. Yet people still consider it to be worth one full dollar. Society accepts this dollar as a medium of exchange, no matter how much the paper itself is worth.

So, our society uses money as a medium of exchange. But what are God's designs for your money?

Money is for giving. Giving to the Lord's work should be our highest priority. Jesus commands, "But seek ye *first* the kingdom of God, and his righteousness; and all these things shall be added unto you" (Matthew 6:33).

When we give, God will provide for our needs. I love these two passages in Proverbs that promise God's provision in response to our giving. Proverbs 28:27 emphasizes, "He that giveth unto the poor shall not lack: but he that hideth his eyes shall have many a curse." Proverbs 3:9–10 reveals an amazing principle: "Honour the Lord with thy substance, and with the firstfruits of all thine increase: So shall thy barns be filled with plenty, and thy presses shall burst out with new wine."

The first thing we should do with the money God entrusts to us is to give. I'm thankful that even before my parents taught me to invest or save, they taught me to give.

When we obey God in this command, He'll bless us. But when we refuse to give to God, we're not obedient. It's impossible to be right with God and wrong with money. Although in the world's eyes we might be well-off, we won't know God's blessings of contentment. By giving to the Lord's work, we demonstrate our priorities and show where our love and allegiance lie.

Money is for living. It seems like so many people are looking for an easy way to make money without working for it. But that's not God's plan.

One of the purposes of money is to provide for our families. Biblically, the husband has the primary responsibility for meeting the financial needs of the family. First Timothy 5:8 says, "But if any provide not for his own, and specially for those of his own house, he hath denied the faith, and is worse than an infidel."

Some people ask, "What if a wife needs to work so we can afford to live at a certain level?" I think if the wife earns money to help make the house payment or the car payment or to buy food, which is the husband's responsibility, he is asking her to help him do his job. It only makes sense then that he help do her jobs—cooking, cleaning, child care, and so forth. It's selfish for a husband to ask his wife to work all day so that they can have a better lifestyle without him consenting to help her at home. If she's assisting him in providing for the family, he needs to reciprocate.

There are circumstances where a husband or father is not in the picture. You may be single, working to provide for yourself. Or you might be a single mom. I have a great deal of respect for single mothers stepping up to provide for their families. Often, they'll work two or even three jobs to take care of their families and then come home to piles of laundry, dishes to wash, meals to make, and homework to help with. That hard work and dedication is a challenge and encouragement to me.

The point is, whether you're a single mom of two, the father of five, or an unmarried twenty-something, your money is means to provide for yourself and, if applicable, your family.

My grandfather reared seven children during the Great Depression. Even though times were incredibly difficult, he absolutely refused to take money from the government. He worked hard to provide for his family his entire life. And that is as it should be. Biblically, men who are physically able to do so should care for their families. In 2 Thessalonians 3:10, Paul wrote, "For even when we were with you, this we commanded you, that if any would not work, neither should he eat."

When Dr. Curtis Hutson left the Forrest Hills Baptist Church to go into evangelism, the pulpit committee called him. They said, "We have interviewed a man who is interested in the position, but he says he can't live on what we were paying you." Dr. Hutson replied, "He probably can't. I never could either. But I wanted to be putting into the church rather than taking out!"

I believe that everyone deserves a fair wage, but I like the heart behind Dr. Hutson's attitude. We want to be giving back all that we can, not seeing how much we can take.

Money is for saving. Have you ever heard the expression, "The money was just burning a hole in my pocket"? It's easy to spend money, but it's also important that we save our money. In fact, the Bible says that it is foolish to spend everything. "There is treasure to be desired and oil in the dwelling of the wise; but a foolish man spendeth it up." (Proverbs 21:20)

Beyond just saving for ourselves, we should also save for future generations. "A good man leaveth an inheritance to his children's children: and the wealth of the sinner is laid up for the just." (Proverbs 13:22).

When my wife's grandmother died, the bulk of her estate went to her three children. But there was also money left in her will for each of her grandchildren. One of the things we did with the money she left my wife was to buy a couch for our home. That couch was special to us. Whenever we saw it, we were reminded of my wife's grandmother and her care in planning for the future.

Some people are naturally thrifty. Saving isn't hard for them. But others struggle with their spending habits. One suggestion to help with saving is looking into a payroll deduction savings plan. If your employer takes it out for you, you don't have to worry about saving money.

You have to pick a plan that works for you. It may be enough for you to predetermine a percentage of money that you're going to save and just set that aside every month. The point is, it's important to save money.

Money is for investing. If you had to list the top ten, twenty, or even thirty topics preached on in most churches, investing your money probably wouldn't make that list. It's not something that I really remember hearing in church as I grew up. But investment is something that the Bible teaches:

> *Then he which had received the one talent came and said, Lord, I knew thee that thou art an hard man, reaping where thou hast*

not sown, and gathering where thou hast not strawed: And I was afraid, and went and hid thy talent in the earth: lo, there thou hast that is thine. His lord answered and said unto him, Thou wicked and slothful servant, thou knewest that I reap where I sowed not, and gather where I have not strawed: Thou oughtest therefore to have put my money to the exchangers, and then at my coming I should have received mine own with usury. Take therefore the talent from him, and give it unto him which hath ten talents. For unto every one that hath shall be given, and he shall have abundance: but from him that hath not shall be taken away even that which he hath. And cast ye the unprofitable servant into outer darkness: there shall be weeping and gnashing of teeth.—MATTHEW 25:24–30

Why was this servant punished? He didn't steal money. He wasn't dishonest. He didn't lose the money. He wasn't even careless. But because he did not invest to earn a return, he was strongly condemned as "wicked," "slothful," and "the unprofitable servant." That condemnation carries an important truth for us.

It is important that we are actively looking for ways to invest our money. Most of us have a steady paycheck that we can plan on receiving. Are we looking for ways to invest a portion of that money? Beyond that, there are times in our lives when we will receive some extra, unexpected money. Perhaps it comes as an income tax refund, an inheritance, or a settlement from an accident or injury. When things like that happen, we have a choice. We could spend all of the money, or we could invest part into something that could pay off for the rest of our lives.

Natural human tendency says to spend money the second we get it. But when we don't invest, we're falling short of God's plan. The clear point of the parable of the talents is to take what God gives us (not just our money, but also our lives) and invest it. The spiritual application of this is the primary truth Jesus was emphasizing when He told the parable. But there is a financial application as well. The Master always expects a return on His investment.

God has specific purposes for how we are to use our money. We should save, invest, and give, to name a few that we've looked at. But if God is so specific about how we should steward our money, why do so many Christians have problems with their finances?

Worrying, Wanting, and Wasting

Money impacts people in a variety of ways. Some take a careful approach and practice all four of the above uses for money. But others let money shape their perspective negatively, and that wrong perspective is portrayed in their actions. I believe that most of those problems can be traced back to one of three wrong attitudes toward money: worry, wanting, and wastefulness. Let's look at all three:

Worrying—Although it is easy to worry about the future, we're commanded not to. Jesus gives us an amazing promise:

> *Therefore take no thought, saying, What shall we eat? or, What shall we drink? or, Wherewithal shall we be clothed? (For after all these things do the Gentiles seek:) for your heavenly Father knoweth that ye have need of all these things. But seek ye first the kingdom of God, and his righteousness; and all these things shall be added unto you. Take therefore no thought for the morrow: for the morrow shall take thought for the things of itself. Sufficient unto the day is the evil thereof.*—MATTHEW 6:31–34

As children of the Heavenly Father, we only have to take our lives one day at a time. God is in control of our future, including our financial future. We can trust Him. When we don't, however, worry begins to show up in destructive ways.

When we worry, we hoard. Proverbs 11:24 describes this: "There is that scattereth, and yet increaseth; and *there is that withholdeth more than is meet, but it tendeth to poverty."*

Have you ever met a professional hoarder? They refuse to part with anything and sometimes won't even buy the basic life necessities. While we may not take our worry to that extreme, we can hoard on a smaller scale. We will not spend our money on anything beyond the basic necessities. We won't give, we won't spend, and we won't invest. God gives us money to use. He doesn't want us to hoard everything we make because we're fearful about the future.

When we worry, we become self-centered. I don't know about you, but I've never struggled to sleep at night wondering how my neighbor would pay his bills. But I think many of us could say that there have been times when it's been hard to sleep because we're worried about our own future. We become so focused on ourselves that we forget about the needs of those around us. Yet Philippians 2:4 says, "Look not every man on his own things, but every man also on the things of others." God isn't pleased or honored when we only focus on ourselves.

When we worry, we decrease our faith. Peter and the rest of the disciples were in the middle of a huge storm. Suddenly, they saw Jesus walking toward them on the water. Peter immediately asked if he could join Jesus.

At first, everything was going well. Imagine the thrill Peter must have felt—he was actually walking on the water.

But then he took his eyes off of Christ. And the second he began to worry about the storm and waves around and below him, he started sinking. Matthew 14:31 says, "And immediately Jesus stretched forth his hand, and caught him, and said unto him, O thou of little faith, wherefore didst thou doubt?"

Worry and faith are opposites. Faith drives away worry; worry chases away faith. When we fear about money, we're actually demonstrating a lack of faith in God.

When we worry, we avoid taking reasonable risks. Part of wise financial planning is taking reasonable risks. We have a responsibility to increase what God has given us—He doesn't want us to bury our money like the unjust steward. There is always a potential that things could go wrong with investments, and because of that, we should be discerning and get wise counsel to make sure the reward outweighs the risk. At the same time, the risk of investment shouldn't paralyze us from not investing at all.

All progress in any area of life involves risk. The great scientist Louis Pasteur received many awards and accolades during his lifetime for his ground-breaking work in medicine. But when they asked him what he wanted inscribed on his tombstone, Pasteur replied, "Joseph Meister lived."

Pasteur was studying immunization for various diseases. He had discovered that weakened forms of different viruses could offer protection against full-blown disease. When nine-year-old Joseph Meister was bitten by a rabid dog, his parents begged Pasteur to test his vaccine on the dying boy. Since Pasteur was not a doctor, he could have been prosecuted for practicing medicine without a license. But he took the risk and began a ten-day injection process that saved the boy's life. When asked for words to sum up a lifetime of work, Pasteur wanted to be remembered for the risk he took that saved a life and would eventually save countless lives.

Worry can cause us to hoard our money and refuse to take risks. It can destroy our faith and cause us to focus only on ourselves.

But that's not the only attitude we can have toward money. Instead of worrying about money, we can start wanting it to the point that it becomes sin.

Wanting—There is nothing wrong with working to have nice things. But when we want those things so much that we become covetous, we're doing wrong. In fact, the Bible says, "He that loveth pleasure shall be a poor man: he that loveth wine and oil shall not be rich" (Proverbs 21:17). Living only for nice things eventually leads to poverty.

There's no guarantee that having nice things will satisfy us. Solomon, one of the wealthiest men in the world, wrote, "He that loveth silver shall not be satisfied with silver; nor he that loveth abundance with increase: this is also vanity" (Ecclesiastes 5:10).

We live in a society that is given over to materialism. Each year billions of dollars are spent on advertising that is designed to create an appetite and desire for things in the hearts and minds of consumers. When we allow our desire for things to control us, we are replacing God. The Bible warns us that "covetousness...is idolatry" (Colossians 3:5). It's likely that we'd never physically bow down to a golden calf, but when we covet, we're doing essentially the same thing.

Excessive wanting and worrying are two opposite attitudes toward money, but they're both dangerous. But in the middle of those two extremes is another attitude that is equally dangerous.

Wasting—Did you get an allowance when you were a child? I remember getting a quarter a week when I was little and rushing to spend it on a candy bar. (I might be dating myself a little with the price.) I thought that the purpose of money was to buy things. I've talked with many adults who have the same attitude toward their spending as I had toward my allowance: money is only for spending. Proverbs 21:20 warns against this attitude: "There is treasure to be desired and oil in the dwelling of the wise; but a foolish man spendeth it up."

We may not *overspend* or want things to the point that we covet. But spending with no thought for the future is an equally poor attitude.

Over the years, I have counseled many people who were struggling with money problems. When we sit down to go over how much of their income they are spending, I almost invariably find that they are simply wasting large amounts of their money. Frankly, that is the result of the same childish attitude I had toward my allowance—I had money, and I wanted to spend it. On a larger scale, rather than carefully planning and budgeting, many people spend on whim and impulse. As a result, they end up either in debt or without any real savings.

Someone once described Americans as "people who spend money they don't have to buy things they don't need to impress people they don't like." I think that's a sadly apt description. We struggle with finances because we don't understand what God says about money and what our attitude toward money should be.

We are accountable to God for how we use those resources. God tells us in Romans 14:12, "So then every one of us shall give account of himself to God." If you let these truths sink into your heart, you'll have a great foundation, not just for the rest of the chapters that we're going to discuss on money, but for life. As Christians, we have a responsibility to steward what God has given us. And part of that responsibility is wisely handling our money.

TEN

DISCOVERING BIBLICAL PRINCIPLES OF FINANCES

It's not how much we have, but what we do with what we have that determines our faithfulness before God. This is true in any area of life—including our finances. One day, we will answer to God for how we handled the resources He entrusted to us.

In our last chapter, we saw that God does tell us in His Word how to handle our money. In this chapter, I'd like to look with you at fifteen practical, biblical principles that should shape our view of personal finances.

Money is a tool—not something we should live for. It is something God has given us so we can live for *Him*.

These principles, while basic, are practical. And they relate to truths we'll cover in the upcoming chapters as well.

1. None of it is yours—it all belongs to God.

> *The silver is mine, and the gold is mine,
> saith the Lord of hosts.*—HAGGAI 2:8

A steward is a person who manages something that does not belong to him. Ultimately, all of our possessions belong to God. When we start to view our money as belonging to us, it changes our attitude toward it. Jesus said to avoid "the deceitfulness of riches" (Matthew 13:22). When we realize God owns everything, it reminds us to be careful of how we take care of what He has entrusted to us.

2. Money is a neutral substance—it can be used for good or evil.

> *For the love of money is the root of all
> evil: which while some coveted after, they
> have erred from the faith, and pierced
> themselves through with many sorrows.*
> —1 TIMOTHY 6:10

Money is neither good nor bad. It is the use or misuse of money that determines its moral value. The *love* of money is the problem, not the money itself. There is no connection between how much money you have and how spiritual you are. Neither riches nor poverty reveal anything about your standing with God.

3. God is against loving riches.

> *For the love of money is the root of all evil: which while some coveted after, they have erred from the faith, and pierced themselves through with many sorrows.*
> —1 TIMOTHY 6:10

One of the temptations of money is that we can allow it to take God's place in our hearts. It is important to heed the Bible's warning when it says "the love of money" is "the root of all evil." Many evil actions and thoughts come from an unhealthy fixation on the devotion to money. It doesn't matter what our economic background is. Rich, poor, or somewhere in the middle, all of us can be tempted to love money.

4. Money can be invested forever, but it can be spent only once.

> *The thoughts of the diligent tend only to plenteousness; but of every one that is hasty only to want.*—PROVERBS 21:5

It is easy to want to spend our paycheck the second we get it. As Bob Jones Sr. once wisely said, however, "Never sacrifice the permanent on the altar of the immediate." It is more fun to spend money, and it is not always wrong to spend money. But once money is spent, it's gone forever.

On the other hand, money that you invest will be working for you for years to come. It is important to keep your long-term priorities and goals in mind when you make your spending and investing decisions.

5. It is sinful to spend more than you have; it is foolish to spend all that you have.

> *There is treasure to be desired and oil in the dwelling of the wise; but a foolish man spendeth it up*—PROVERBS 21:20.

When you buy something you cannot afford, you are presuming on God and the future. With the click of a mouse, the tap of a screen, or the swipe of a card, you can have almost anything you want immediately. But that can be dangerous. You should not buy things on credit cards with installment loans that you will not be able to pay off just so you can have them now. Wisdom says that you should never spend all of the money that you make.

6. Most financial problems can be traced to ignorance, indulgence, or irresponsibility.

> *He that loveth pleasure shall be a poor man: he that loveth wine and oil shall not be rich.*—PROVERBS 21:17

Many people do not grow up in homes where money management is taught. When they get their first job, they have no idea what to do with their first paycheck. If you're not familiar with wise financial principles, start learning now. Other people, however, struggle with finances, not because they don't know the truth, but because they're indulgent in their spending. You cannot expect to prosper if you are focused on satisfying your appetites with your purchases. Some people have to have the latest car, the best television, the trendiest clothes, or the biggest house. While spending money feels good, indulgently spending money isn't wise. In fact, it's a form of irresponsibility. While you might have nice things, those irresponsible choices will haunt you in the future.

7. God expects us to increase what He gives us.

> *Thou oughtest therefore to have put my money to the exchangers, and then at my coming I should have received mine own with usury.*—MATTHEW 25:27

For years, I knew this was true spiritually. I knew to take advantage of my opportunities in the spiritual realm and make the most of every one of them. But when I studied the Bible more thoroughly, I realized that the same principle holds in the financial world. God is looking for a return on His investment in us. We need to be wise in how we handle our money, recognizing that God expects us to be just as faithful and diligent with our money as we are with our talents and spiritual gifts.

8. God is against "get-rich-quick" schemes.

> *He that hasteth to be rich hath an evil eye,*
> *and considereth not that poverty shall come*
> *upon him.*—PROVERBS 28:22

Many people are looking for a shortcut or an easy way to get rich. God is never behind schemes like that. I know several preachers who have suffered huge financial losses because they got on board with a financial scheme that they thought would be the answer to all of their financial needs. The plans, programs, and systems you see on television are not the answer to your money problems. When you think about it, if those plans really worked, the people selling them would be using them for themselves rather than selling you a product.

9. God is against trusting riches.

> *Charge them that are rich in this world,*
> *that they be not highminded, nor trust*
> *in uncertain riches, but in the living God,*
> *who giveth us richly all things to enjoy.*
> —1 TIMOTHY 6:17

If we're wise, we'll save and invest our money. Yet that carries with it a danger—we can begin to trust money more than we trust God. Because we've saved up enough money, we feel as if we don't really need to ask God to provide for us because we've got it covered. Paul instructed Timothy to warn the rich not to trust in "uncertain riches." Money is no guarantee of security or happiness, and those who trust in it will always be disappointed.

10. God is not against riches.

> *Charge them that are rich in this world, that they be not highminded, nor trust in uncertain riches, but in the living God, who giveth us richly all things to enjoy.*
> —1 TIMOTHY 6:17

God wants us to enjoy what He has given us. Although God does command us not to *love* money, He is not against money itself. In fact, His plan for funding His work in this world depends on the giving of His children. He is pleased when you have money as long as the money does not really have you. The Bible is very clear that God gives us good things, including money, with the intention that we enjoy them.

11. The more you spend when you are young, the less you have available when you are old.

> *There is treasure to be desired and oil in the dwelling of the wise; but a foolish man spendeth it up.*—PROVERBS 21:20

If we're willing to defer the purchase of things until we can pay for them, we'll be better off financially. It's not wrong to have nice things—there's nothing spiritual about sitting on milk crates in a rented house. (I like having a comfortable couch to relax on.) But as you're first starting out, you may have to live with things like hand-me-down furniture.

12. Spending should be deferred; giving should not.

> *But seek ye first the kingdom of God, and his righteousness; and all these things shall be added unto you.*—MATTHEW 6:33

A common philosophy among Christians is to wait until you've made it financially to give. But there's a problem with that approach. Giving is primarily a spiritual decision, not a financial one. On your scale of priorities, saving and investing should always come after giving. That is the principle Jesus was describing in Matthew 6:33. Don't take God's money to put in your investment. If God puts on your heart to give more, do it, even if it means less money to save and invest. God blesses those who put Him first.

13. Wealth and poverty are equally dangerous.

> *Remove far from me vanity and lies: give me neither poverty nor riches; feed me with food convenient for me: Lest I be full, and deny thee, and say, Who is the* Lord? *or lest I be poor, and steal, and take the name of my God in vain.*—Proverbs 30:8–9

There is danger in both extreme wealth and extreme poverty. Either can damage our attitude toward God. Extreme wealth can tempt us to forget about God and how dependent we are on Him. Extreme poverty, on the other hand, can make us fear the future and do things we normally wouldn't do. It can tempt us to forget that God has promised to supply our need. No matter what our financial state is, we need the Lord in our lives.

14. You must pay for every purchase; wise people pay when they purchase.

> *The rich ruleth over the poor, and the borrower is servant to the lender.*
> —Proverbs 22:7

Many offers today depend on making people think that they will not have to pay for what they buy. The zero-interest plans and deferred-payment options encourage you to buy things that you cannot afford by making you feel like you do not need to pay for them. Everything that you buy must be paid for eventually. It is far better for you to pay when you make the purchase rather than financing it and still be making payments long after the item is used up and gone.

15. Money is not what life is about.

> *And he said unto them, Take heed, and beware of covetousness: for a man's life consisteth not in the abundance of the things which he possesseth.*—LUKE 12:15

I remember preaching for a special meeting in a small church. The pastor put me in a small motor lodge in the town, explaining that the nearest big, chain hotel was thirty minutes away, and that the motor lodge was the best place the town had to offer. That night, I got a good night's sleep—I had everything I needed. But then the pastor told me about the preacher they'd had a few months ago. He refused to stay at the small hotel and insisted on being put in the big hotel thirty minutes away. This pastor had the wrong view of money.

Money should never be our highest goal in life. There is so much more to life than earning, spending, and saving money. True satisfaction comes when we find God's will for our lives and pursue it with our whole hearts.

ELEVEN

DEFEATING THE ENEMY OF DEBT

When my wife and I first married, we didn't have many discussions about money. That's because we didn't have any money to discuss. Everything we made went to the basics—tithe, food, housing, insurance, and things necessary to survival.

I remember the day we got our first credit card. For the first few months, it was a liberating experience. I didn't have to wait until I had enough money to buy a new shirt and tie—I could get it all on my credit card and worry about paying for it later. That credit card soon became a very good friend of mine…and then it became a significant enemy.

We never went deeply into debt. My big credit card bill in those days totaled $500. But I was making $110 a week. To me, that $500 represented more than a month's salary. To compound the problem, that wasn't the only debt I had.

We had a car, but it was so beat up it barely ran. My father-in-law drove it once, and he was appalled. He said, "I don't want my daughter riding in that car. Find out how much it will take to make the down payment on a decent car, and I'll loan it to you."

He loaned us $500, and we put it down on a $3,000 car, financing the rest. Although we paid him back for the down payment in a year, we still had the car loan. Now, we had to pay that on top of the credit card payment each month.

Then, I found a motorcycle. For just $24 a month, I could ride in style. So we added that to our budget as well. Before long, it was all I could do to make the payments each month. I had fallen into the typical "buy now, pay later" mentality that dominates American society.

After I had been a pastor for a couple of years, I realized that I wasn't honoring God with my finances. I made a commitment to my wife that we were going to get out of debt. With His help, we paid off every penny that we owed.

A large number of Americans struggle with debt. Take a look at these sobering statistics:

- The average American household is $139,500 in debt.
- The average student that has gone to or graduated from college owes above $49,000.
- The average American household has $5,000 in credit card debt.
- Combined consumer debt in America is over $1.3 trillion.[1]

Even Christians, the people that should be setting an example for the lost world, easily fall into heavy debt. Yet that shouldn't be so. As believers, we have an obligation to be good stewards of the money God has entrusted to us.

Why We Struggle with Debt

When my wife and I made the decision to get out of debt, it wasn't an immediate release. It took a plan, time, and lots of work. Honestly, there were times when I wasn't sure our plan was going to work. There were many moments when I wanted to quit, and I made several mistakes. But the struggle was worth it, and the day finally came when my wife and I paid our last payment and were officially debt free.

---

[1] Larry Alton, "Household Debt Is Enslaving Americans," *Nasdaq.com*, May 22, 2017, https://www.nasdaq.com/article/household-debt-is-enslaving-americans-cm793135 (accessed June 10, 2018).

You might be able to relate to our story. Or you may not really struggle with debt. You might be somewhere in between, or know someone who could use some financial counsel. Wherever you are on your financial journey, I believe that the biblical principles we'll cover in the next few pages will encourage and challenge you as you grow in the area of stewardship.

As we look at how to get out of debt, there are two basic principles to keep in mind. First, the Bible has a negative view of debt. Proverbs 22:7 says, "The rich ruleth over the poor, and the borrower is servant to the lender." If you've ever been in debt, you can relate. When every penny you earn is already promised to someone else, you are no better off than a slave because nothing you have really belongs to you.

Second, you need to understand the psychology behind debt. One reason I think many people are in debt is, whether they recognize it or not, the motivation of greed. It's easy and even natural to start thinking we have to have the newest item, the latest fashion, or the most expensive model. We see what our friends and neighbors have, and we want it. But this consuming desire for material things sets us on the path to financial instability. In fact, it will ultimately destroy us.

Part of the reason for this is because of the depreciating nature of things and the accumulating upkeep they require. For example, that new car is great when you first buy it, but after a few years, the car will start costing you more than just gas and insurance. It may need a new exhaust system, new tires, or a tune up. That car, boat, new appliance—you name it—that you bought to serve you starts requiring more money usually before you have even finished paying for it. Before you make that new purchase, ask yourself if you can afford the upkeep. In other words, can you master the purchase, or will the purchase master you?

Debt, once it gets its grip on us, can become so suffocating that it causes depression. I've counseled people so deeply in debt that they felt there was no hope they would ever get out. The devil can use debt to rob us of the joy and pleasure God wants us to experience.

I like to compare getting out of debt to dieting. I like being skinny—at least what I remember of it. The way my clothes fit, the fact that my knees didn't hurt, and the extra energy I had was wonderful. But I also like eating. I like candy bars, thick steaks and baked potatoes with butter and sour cream, and French fries with cheese and barbeque sauce. I just like food! When I'm fat, I enjoy eating. When I'm skinny, I enjoy the benefits of being skinny.

The problem is that there is a long road between fat and skinny. And to make the trip, you have to endure a period of time when you can't enjoy eating because of the diet, but you can't enjoy being skinny because, well, you aren't skinny yet. That middle period is my least favorite time. But whether it's with dieting or budgeting, it's impossible to get from where you are now to where you want to be without denying yourself things you're accustomed to.

It is fun to buy things, even if you can't afford them. But that pleasure doesn't begin to compare with the joy of being out of debt. If we're honest with ourselves, the temporary thrill we get with buying new things doesn't make up for worrying over past-due bills.

In contrast, the person who is free from debt has the pleasure of paying bills when they are due without worrying about where the money will come from. He also avoids paying exorbitant interest on his purchases.

In this chapter, we're going to cover some principles on getting out of debt. But foundational to everything else in this chapter is this—you will never get out of debt if you are not willing to go through the process of denying things you want but don't need.

The plan I'm going to share with you isn't instant or painless, but for me, it was the path to financial freedom. Just as with dieting, you can't succeed by taking shortcuts. It will take hard work and some denial.

I have encouraged many couples over the years to use this plan, and I've never yet had a couple who put in the time and stuck to the plan come back to me and say it didn't work.

I believe that if you stick to these steps, it will work for you too.

Creating a Budget

To get out of debt, you need a game plan. When it comes to finances, that game plan is called a *budget.*

Many people, especially those who are in debt, don't like the idea of budgeting because it feels restrictive. In reality, however, a budget is freeing because it allows you to develop a reasonable and workable plan to get out of debt. If you don't know where your money is going or how you need to be spending it, it'll be tough to get out of debt.

Furthermore, budgeting isn't as difficult as you might assume. It's actually a very straightforward process:

Make a list of all monthly bills and regular expenses. Statistics reveal that less than 8 percent of American families have a written spending plan.[2] Part of the poor financial state Americans are in can be directly related to this number. You need to know where your money is currently going before you can start paying down on your debt, and to do so, you have to make a list of all monthly bills and regular expenses.

A common mistake budgeting newcomers make is only including the monthly bills they receive. But you have additional expenses. For example, if you pay your insurance every quarter or twice a year, don't forget to include it in your budget, dividing your premiums by

---

[2] "Personal Finance Statistics," *Debt.com,* https://www.debt.com/edu/personal-finance-statistics/ (accessed October 17, 2018).

how many months fall between each payment. And while you don't get a bill from the grocery store, that's a regular recurring expense you need to plan for. And of course, your tithe, missions, or other giving also will not be billed, but it should be included in your budget.

Budgeting shouldn't be unnecessarily overwhelming. Don't try to create a separate category for every minor expense. For example, you don't need one category for shirts and one category for shoes. Have categories that are broad enough to not be cumbersome, but clear enough that you can keep track of where everything is going.

Divide each monthly obligation by the number of pay periods per month. Add up your list of monthly expenses, and divide by how often you receive income. If you get paid monthly, divide by one. If you get paid twice a month or every two weeks, divide by two. If you get paid every week, divide by four, and so on.

Add up the total obligations per pay period and compare the sum to your take-home pay. Step three often causes a bit of shock. I know that was the case for my wife and me and many other couples I've counseled. For the first time, you may be seeing why you're having trouble making ends meet. If you are spending more than you make, you'll naturally fall into debt.

Make necessary adjustments. This step is critical. Now that you know what you have to spend every month, make necessary adjustments. If your income does not equal your obligations, you are going to have to decrease spending, increase your income, or both. This may mean getting an extra job or working overtime. It may mean cutting out the "fun stuff" in your budget that isn't strictly necessary. For example, you don't need cable television or a Netflix subscription. You don't need to eat out several nights in the week. You have to make a total mental shift. Just because everyone else has something doesn't mean that you need it too. Your goal right now is to do everything you can to get your monthly spending under budget.

Begin a budget notebook, either on paper or on the computer. It's time to start tracking. Pick a program that works best for you. There are several online apps that work well, or you could simply document your spending in a spreadsheet. In fact, you could even keep track on paper. Whatever you choose, keep it simple. Make deposits into each account every time you get paid. Whatever amount you have allocated for your tithe and giving, mortgage, car payment, credit card payments, groceries, and so forth should be credited to that item in the budget. Keep this record just like the register in your checkbook.

Set up a surplus account. If your budget is done properly, there should be at least a little money left over each time you get paid. Even if it is only ten or twenty dollars, record that amount in the surplus category.

Record your expenses every time you spend the money. Write down the expenditure against the money that you have already credited to that account and "withdraw" it from the account when you write the check.

Spend only the extra money in your surplus or miscellaneous account for things that are not in your budget. Just having money in your bank account doesn't mean it's available to spend—it may be committed to payments that are coming up. The only money that is free for spending is whatever is in the surplus account. You only have what is not owed.

If you stick to this plan, you will not be incurring new debt. This is the first step to getting out of debt.

Paying down Your Debt

But what do you do about the old debt? How do you pay that down?

Analyze your credit card habits. Credit cards can be useful tools, and I'm not against them. In fact, I have a credit card that I use. But my wife and I pay it off in full every month to avoid interest charges.

If you're struggling with debt, try this. The first time when you have a month that you don't pay the credit card bill in full, put the credit card in a drawer. Don't take it out again until the bill is paid off—no exceptions. The second time you don't pay it off, it's time for more drastic measures. Take a pair of scissors and cut the card into little pieces.

You can't empty a sink with a cup unless you first turn off the water, and you can't get rid of debt until you stop adding additional debt.

Credit cards are tempting, and marketers know this. Did you know that the average American adult receives seven credit card solicitations each year? (I think I get seven each month!) There is an enormous industry dedicated to getting you to use credit cards foolishly. My challenge to you is not to succumb to the pressure, no matter how tempting it can be.

Be aware of the quarterly windfall. If you get paid weekly, you will have an extra paycheck four times a year. (If you get paid every two weeks, it will happen twice a year.) Your grocery, gas, giving, and a few other accounts won't change, and you'll spend that money as usual. But your monthly mortgage, car payments and credit card payments are already covered by the other paychecks. Don't spend that money—put it towards your debt.

Pick one bill on which to pay extra. Take the money that is left from your monthly categories and put it toward an extra payment on the principle of the smallest bill you owe (or the one that is scheduled to be paid off the quickest). For example, we started with the motorcycle payment. Since that was just $24 per month, it wasn't too hard to add $24 and pay extra toward that bill each month. Just by putting our extra money toward that bill, we paid the total off in less than half the time the loan was originally set to run. By paying early, we also eliminated some of the interest, saving us even more money.

When that bill is paid off, add the amount you have been paying on it to another bill. We added the $48 we had been paying on the motorcycle to our regular payment for the next bill. As I recall, that payment was around $70. With the added money, we were paying $118 each month on that account. We continued that same process until we had paid off all of the debt we had accumulated.

The advantage of this method is that, while it takes dedication, it generally doesn't require a drastic lifestyle change. In my case, it required us to come up with an additional $24 per month to get started. Then we just continued using the money we had been spending to pay down the total until we were done. This process gains momentum with every payment. Before long, the results you begin to see will encourage you in sticking to the plan. If you faithfully continue the process, you'll be amazed at how quickly you get ahead.

You've Made It—Now What?

The day has finally come. You've finally paid off that last loan, and you are officially debt free. Congratulations!

But what's next? How can you be sure that you won't fall back into debt? How do you wisely adjust to this new lifestyle of debt-free living?

Learn to purchase wisely. Even when you're out of debt, keep your budget. This will help you to avoid those impulse buys that can drag you right back into debt. While you should allocate some spending money for "fun" things, make sure that it still fits in your budget.

Now that you're not paying off bills and loans, don't spend that extra money on only unnecessary things. Start thinking toward making bigger wise investments. For example, one of the biggest purchases you will make is buying a home. If you think ahead to the future, your home could be one of your best investments.

Pay cash. The average American spends $1.22 for every $1.00 he earns. This is an easy trap to fall into, but it isn't a wise one. The rule to avoiding this is simple in theory but a little more difficult in practice: if you do not have the money to pay for something, wait. If you do use your credit card to purchase something, deduct that amount from your checking account balance then, rather than waiting until you actually write the check to pay the bill. Doing so will make it easy to pay the bill in full when it comes due. Always keep in mind that the purpose of a credit card is not to allow you to buy things you can't pay off in full at the end of the month.

Wait for nonessential items to go on sale. When I needed a new suit some time back, I waited for a sale instead of buying one right away. As a result, I got a well-made suit for $300 less. I wanted the best value for my money, and the on-sale suit I bought was made better, looked better, and would last longer. If you're willing to practice patience, you'll get better quality at a better price—every time.

Check the internet. With a little searching, you can find some amazing deals on the internet. Major internet shopping sites can help you potentially find something much cheaper than you could locally. Look at other options to make sure you're getting the best possible deal.

Don't let your car drive you into the ground. With the exception of credit card spending, people waste and lose more money on cars than on anything else. As the price of cars has gone up, the length of car loans has grown as well. Once, it was rare to see a car loan that was longer than three years. Now it is not at all uncommon for car loans to run seven or even eight years. And think about this—the average car loan payment is $523.[3]

Most of us will reach some point in our lives where we can afford a new car without struggling to make any payments. Yet when we reach that point, we shouldn't look at it as an automatic reason to go buy a new car. When I reached that "I-can-buy-a-new-car" stage in my life, I still drove a nine-year-old Lincoln Town Car. It was a beautiful car that rode well and was in excellent condition. I got it

---

[3] Phil LeBeau, "A $523 Monthly Loan Payment Is the New Standard for U.S. Car Buyers," *Usatoday.com*, May 31, 2018, https://www.usatoday.com/story/money/cars/2018/05/31/average-car-buyer-now-paying-523-monthly-loan-payment/658873002/ (accessed October 17, 2018).

at an estate sale for just over $5,900 when it had 41,000 miles on it. New, the car cost nearly $50,000. So for about 12 percent of the original cost, I got roughly two-thirds of the useful life of the car.

If you currently have debt on a car, my suggestion is to keep the car until the debt is paid off rather than trading it in and adding on more debt. When it is paid for, try to drive it at least one year longer. During this year, deposit the payment you would have made on a car directly into a savings account. That will greatly increase the amount you have to put down on your next car.

Take out as short of a loan as you can when you purchase the next car. The monthly payments on a shorter loan are higher, but because you will have your old car for a trade-in and one year's worth of payments saved up, your payments should not be a burden. Repeat this process once or twice, and you will be able to drive out of the dealership— the used car dealership—without a payment book.

Unattach yourself from things. Materialism is a pull for all of us. Recently, I read an author who believed that consumerism and its attending debt are to our generation what slavery was to Christians of the eighteenth and nineteenth centuries in the sense that it is an obvious sin except to those who practice it, and all of us can fall prey to it. As Christians, we have to remember that it is God's money and not ours that we are wasting in the pursuit and accumulation of things that are only temporal.

I recall reading that only 6 percent of Bible-believing Christians tithe regularly.[4] The average Christian gives less than 4 percent of his income to God.[5] What a sobering commentary on our values and priorities! When our thinking is things-centered, our eyes get off of God and His bigger purpose and onto how we can satisfy ourselves.

Stewardship Evaluation

We've been walking through a plan to get out of debt. My goal is to help you get the peace of mind that comes with financial freedom. But while getting out of debt is wonderful, I want you to understand the larger principle behind it. We should be careful with our finances, not just so that we can live with peace of mind, but so we can be good stewards of the money God has entrusted to us. We're to be faithful in what God has given us. "Let a man so account of us, as of the ministers of Christ, and stewards of the mysteries of God. Moreover it is required in stewards, that a man be found faithful" (1 Corinthians 4:1-2). We are to occupy until Jesus comes. "And he called his ten servants, and delivered them ten pounds, and said unto them, Occupy till I come" (Luke 19:13).

---

[4] Randy Alcorn, *Money, Possessions, and Eternity* (Tyndale House Publishers, 2003), Kindle location 169.
[5] Ibid., Kindle location 3928.

After reading this chapter, ask yourself, "Am I a wise steward?" Put yourself to the test below. The following characteristics are good starting points to check how you are currently doing as a steward of the resources God has given to you. Look at your own life in light of these five stewards and see which one most closely matches where you are right now.

Smart Steward

- Pays all his bills on time
- Has no consumer debt
- Has one to two month's income in the bank as a cushion
- Is investing for the future beyond Social Security or pension
- Gives generously

Steady Steward

- Pays all his bills on time
- Has little or no consumer debt with the exception of a car loan
- Has one to four week's income in the bank as a cushion
- Has only Social Security or a pension for retirement
- Gives faithfully (tithes and an occasional offering)

Shaky Steward

- Pays most of his bills on time, but is late on one or more each month

- Has consumer debt excluding car totaling 10–15 percent of take-home pay

- Has no cushion for emergencies

- Has only Social Security or a pension for retirement

- Gives sporadically and robs God frequently (tithes occasionally)

Sinking Steward

- Is late on one-third or more of his bills each month

- Consumer debt excluding car totals 15 percent or more of take-home pay

- Has no cushion for emergencies and charges gas and food on a credit card

- Has only Social Security or a pension for retirement and may have borrowed against his pension

- Seldom if ever gives and robs God regularly

Sunken Steward

- Has items that are being repossessed

- Is facing reorganization or bankruptcy

- Is a reproach and a bad testimony as a Christian

- Experiences remorse over his situation. This can lead to repentance, repaying, rebuilding, and rejoicing; or relief by buying something else he cannot afford, repetition in continuing his spending habits, and ruin.

After evaluating yourself, maybe you've realized that you are a smart or steady steward. If that's the case, keep doing what you've been doing. Or maybe you're not where you want to be. If that's the case, remember that today is a new start. Make a commitment to yourself and to God that you are going to begin being a wise financial steward. Determine today to follow the steps above in getting out of debt and staying out of it. Seek out a wise counselor for accountability. With hard work, dedication, and the Lord's help, you can do it.

TWELVE

PREPARING FOR THE FUTURE

George Whitefield, the powerful evangelist, traveled back and forth between England and America preaching the gospel to sometimes thousands at once and spreading revival. His ministry was incredibly effective. During his seventh and final trip to America, he stopped in Massachusetts. One evening, some people came to the house where he was staying and asked him to speak to them for a little while from the Bible. Whitefield lit a candle and told them he would "preach till the candle burned out." When the message was done, Whitefield went to bed and died in his sleep.

I love preaching, just as George Whitefield did. In fact, I think it would be incredible to one day when I'm older, after an evening of preaching, go to bed and wake up in Heaven. But I don't know if that's the plan God has for me. Years ago, I realized that income as a pastor will not be covered by the Social Security system. That means that if I reach an age when I cannot preach regularly anymore, there will be nothing, humanly speaking, on which I can live.

About the time I realized that, I was also learning from businessmen and reading about investing in real estate. Finally, I talked to another pastor about my situation. At that point, we both had basically zero net worth. We didn't owe anything, but we didn't own anything either. My friend encouraged me to make wise plans for the future. I needed to find a way to fulfill the obligation I had to provide for my family and leave something for my children and future grandchildren.

Planning for the future doesn't equal a lack of faith. I know the Lord loves me and promises to take care of me. At the same time, none of that absolves me of my responsibility to plan. In fact, in one of the most famous passages in Proverbs, God emphasizes this principle.

The virtuous woman in Proverbs 31 was not an average housewife. It appears that her husband was wealthy, and as a result, she managed a large household. She oversaw her servants and made sure her house ran smoothly. Today, we might say that she had a lot on her plate. To succeed, she had to be organized. She knew that, as the old saying goes, to fail to plan is to plan to fail.

This woman trusted the Lord but was also rightly focused on the future. In the description we are given of her life, I believe we find seven crucial elements that made her successful in managing finances.

The Proverbs 31 woman was diligent. In God's economy, there is no substitute for good, old-fashioned hard work. Thomas Edison said, "Genius is 1 percent inspiration and 99 percent perspiration."

> *She seeketh wool, and flax, and worketh willingly with her hands. She is like the merchants' ships; she bringeth her food from afar. She riseth also while it is yet night, and giveth meat to her household, and a portion to her maidens. She looketh well to the ways of her household, and eateth not the bread of idleness.*—PROVERBS 31:13–15, 27

From Scripture, we get the impression that this woman was talented but also a hard worker. Because she had so much to do and so many responsibilities, she got up early and diligently completed her tasks. She had servants to help her, but she also worked with her own hands. She didn't expect others to do her work for her. Hard work is really a foundational requirement to increasing your financial assets.

The Proverbs 31 woman was an investor. The virtuous woman was a wise businesswoman.

> *She considereth a field, and buyeth it:*
> *with the fruit of her hands she planteth a*
> *vineyard.*—PROVERBS 31:16

This woman was wealthy in her own right, but she didn't just spend money on anything she wanted. She could have bought a new wardrobe, a chariot, or expensive jewelry. Instead, after careful consideration, she bought a field to use as a vineyard and plants to fill the field. This is forward thinking. Typically, it takes three years before grapevines produce enough grapes to be commercially useful. She used the money she made to do something that would make even more money in the future.

Investing may require patience and foresight, but as the Proverbs 31 woman reveals in her story, it's worth it.

The Proverbs 31 woman was discerning. She wasn't gullible or naïve, and she understood the value of the things that she made.

> *She perceiveth that her merchandise is*
> *good: her candle goeth not out by night.*
> —PROVERBS 31:18

A smooth-talking merchant couldn't convince her to sell him products for less than they were worth. What she sold was high quality, and she was willing to stay up late to make sure that everything was done properly. She made sure that she was on top of everything that was going on.

Before making an investment, spend time becoming educated about what exactly you're putting your money into. Putting your money in an investment you haven't thought through often backfires. To put it this way, someone once said, "There is a difference between education and experience. You get an education when you read the fine print; you get experience when you don't!"

The Proverbs 31 woman was generous. At first, this almost seems contradictory. Why would we give money away when we're trying to prepare for the future? Let's look back to the virtuous woman.

> *She stretcheth out her hand to the poor; yea,*
> *she reacheth forth her hands to the needy.*
> —PROVERBS 31:20

In Bible times, beggars reached out toward people walking by and asked for money. But rather than waiting for people to reach out to her, the virtuous woman reached out to them. She was looking for opportunities to be generous.

The purpose of investing is not solely to pile up money. In fact, successful investing increases our resources and thereby gives us the ability to meet the needs of others. It allows us the chance to give to the Lord's work. In addition, it helps us to guard against selfishness. Planning to give to others helps make sure that our money and investments will not gain control of our hearts and minds.

The Proverbs 31 woman looked for the best investment, not the least expensive. Notice how the virtuous woman clothes her household.

> *She is not afraid of the snow for her household: for all her household are clothed with scarlet. She maketh herself coverings of tapestry; her clothing is silk and purple.*
> —PROVERBS 31:21–22

Always consider the quality of the item you're purchasing, not just the cost. The Proverbs 31 woman certainly did. Often, there is a definite difference in quality that is worth an extra cost.

Don't cut corners just to save money. For example, if you are investing in stocks, buy a company that is worth owning. If you are looking at land, buy a piece of land that will one day be worth something. Someone said, "The bitterness of poor quality lingers long after the sweetness of low price is forgotten."

The Proverbs 31 woman was wise. Wisdom is more than knowledge; it is the proper application of knowledge.

> *She openeth her mouth with wisdom; and in her tongue is the law of kindness.*
> —PROVERBS 31:26

Seeing things from a godly perspective helps you make the right decisions when you face choices in your life—decisions that not only impress and please people, but decisions that please God.

Any successful plan for the future requires wisdom. Dangers and risks are involved in every investment, but wisdom helps you avoid pitfalls and recover from reversals or setbacks. Ask God for wisdom as you develop a money management plan.

The Proverbs 31 woman was kind. When you think of a key to business success, you probably don't immediately think of kindness. As the Proverbs 31 woman shows us, however, kindness is something all of us should develop, no matter what our occupation is.

> She openeth her mouth with wisdom;
> and in her tongue is the law of kindness.
> —PROVERBS 31:26

Sometimes, you may need to make a firm decision or hold your ground over a business deal. But always be kind.

The virtuous woman wasn't mastered by money, but she did use it as a tool in her day-to-day life. This should be our approach as well. Let the Proverbs 31 woman's example encourage you as you develop your own financial plan.

The Importance of Hard Work

John Smith was a famous colonial leader in early American history. When he became governor of Jamestown, the colony was in bad shape. One of his most famous policies was the rule that if a man refused to work, he should not eat. After implementing this policy, the colony greatly improved.[1] Smith recognized the biblical principle in 2 Thessalonians 3:10.

> *For even when we were with you, this we commanded you, that if any would not work, neither should he eat. For we hear that there are some which walk among you disorderly, working not at all, but are busybodies. Now them that are such we command and exhort by our Lord Jesus Christ, that with quietness they work, and eat their own bread.*
> —2 THESSALONIANS 3:10–12

God's plan is for those that can work, to work. Certainly we recognize that there are those who cannot work for themselves. We are supposed to care for the aged, the sick, the widows, and orphans. But there is no plan in the Bible for feeding people who could but would not work. Working is an integral part of any Bible-based money management system.

God commends labor. Proverbs 14:23 tells us that "in all labour there is profit: but the talk of the lips tendeth only to penury." No matter if you work in an air-conditioned

---

[1] "The Life of John Smith," *Nps.gov*, https://www.nps.gov/jame/learn/historyculture/life-of-john-smith.htm (accessed June 10, 2018).

office, a classroom, the medical field, the food business, or do heavy manual labor, there is profit in work.

We've heard stories of those in the army who were ordered to take a stack of bricks one at a time and move them to the other side of the drill area. After they were finally done, they would be ordered to reverse the process and move them back to where they were in the first place. At first, this doesn't make sense, but there is a purpose to it. The drill instructors are teaching discipline, obedience to orders, and hard work. Those are qualities that every soldier (and every Christian) needs to be successful. Hard work, no matter what form, is always valuable.

Years ago, my daughter was in a doctrines class in our Christian school. I was helping her go over one of her assignments and saw that they were studying Sabellianism, an ancient heresy concerning the Trinity.

My wife asked, "Why are they studying such an in-depth topic?"

Jokingly, I replied, "Because the teacher hates them!"

In truth, there was value in what she was studying. Almost all false doctrine can be traced back to errors in the early church. The more we understand those errors, the better protected we are from false doctrine. But besides the content of what she was learning, I'm thankful my daughter took difficult classes in high school, for I believe choosing them better prepared her for life as an adult.

No matter what job you hold or what task you're assigned, do your best. There is profit in all labor because work is a gift from God.

In fact, God places such a high priority on labor that He condemns laziness. Ultimately, the lazy person will end up with nothing: "The soul of the sluggard desireth, and hath nothing: but the soul of the diligent shall be made fat" (Proverbs 13:4).

Those who don't work hard want the same things hard-working people want. They begin to covet and desire things they could have but refuse to work for. As you read through this passage from Proverbs, notice how the slothful man excuses his actions.

> I went by the field of the slothful, and by the
> vineyard of the man void of understanding;
> And, lo, it was all grown over with thorns, and
> nettles had covered the face thereof, and the
> stone wall thereof was broken down. Then I
> saw, and considered it well: I looked upon it,
> and received instruction. Yet a little sleep, a
> little slumber, a little folding of the hands to
> sleep: So shall thy poverty come as one that
> travelleth; and thy want as an armed man.
> —PROVERBS 24:30–34

In his devotional *Morning and Evening*, Charles Spurgeon wrote,

The worst of sluggards only ask for a *little* slumber; they would be indignant if they were accused of thorough idleness. A little folding of the hands to sleep is all they crave, and they have a crowd of reasons to show that this indulgence is a very proper one. Yet by these *littles* the day ebbs out, and the time for labour is all gone, and the field is grown over with thorns.

It is by *little* procrastinations that men ruin their souls. They have no intention to delay for years—a few months will bring the more convenient season. Tomorrow, if you will, they will attend to serious things; but the present hour is so occupied and altogether so unsuitable, that they beg to be excused. Like sands from an hourglass, time passes, life is wasted by driblets, and seasons of grace are lost by *little* slumbers."[2]

As Spurgeon aptly describes, the lazy man doesn't look at his actions as "that bad." Eventually, he tells himself he'll work hard and accomplish what he needs to…just not right now.

---

[2] Charles Spurgeon, *Morning and Evening* (Start Publishing LLC, 2012), evening reading for November 24.

God wants us to be actively working. There's so much truth to the old adage, "Never put off till tomorrow what can be done today." Procrastinating, at its heart, is a form of laziness. God wants us to work hard now as we prepare for the future.

The Importance of Investing

When I was a young pastor, I would say, "I would rather give my money away than save it, because God pays better interest than the Second National Bank." There is some truth to that thinking. I'm grateful that I learned about tithing and giving from a young age. I've asked the Lord to help me give more every year, for I believe that giving is more important than saving and investing. But that doesn't mean that saving and investing has no importance whatsoever.

In Matthew 25, we see the parable Jesus told about the servants and the talents. Each man was given a different number of talents, depending on his ability. The man who was given five talents gained five more talents, and the man who was given two talents gained two more talents. Although the amount of return was different, the rate was the same. Each received the same commendation from the master.

But the servant who was given one talent was rebuked. He hid his talent so that he would not lose it, but he gained nothing. It's not as if he did something *wrong* with his money—he didn't steal or waste his master's money. He didn't make worthless investments or frivolously spend it. He kept everything that he had been given by his master to the point of wrapping the talent so it wouldn't be damaged by its burial in the ground.

The key to the story is recognizing that the servants weren't just charged with keeping what they had been given. If that's all the master wanted, he could have taken the money with him. They were charged to produce something in his absence so that when the master returned, he would have more than he did when he left. When the servant with one talent didn't do so, he received harsh condemnation.

> *His lord answered and said unto him, Thou wicked and slothful servant, thou knewest that I reap where I sowed not, and gather where I have not strawed: Thou oughtest therefore to have put my money to the exchangers, and then at my coming I should have received mine own with usury. Take therefore the talent from him, and give it unto him which hath ten talents. For unto every one that hath shall be given, and he shall have abundance: but from him that hath not shall be taken away even that which he hath.*—MATTHEW 25:26–29

Wise investors put their money where it makes more money. God, the wisest investor of all, does this. When we demonstrate that we are faithful with what He has already given to us, He gives us more to produce and even greater results. This is true in the spiritual realm, but it's also true in the physical realm.

If God wants us to increase what we have been given like the first two servants, how do we do that?

Steps to Prepare for the Future

As you begin thinking about the future, here are a few things to consider.

It's wise to save a cushion for emergencies. By that, I mean try to have one to three month's of your salary laid aside. Life happens. You might lose your job or have an unexpected car repair. If you do not have something in reserve, when an emergency happens, your financial plan will get derailed.

Not having that emergency cushion can force you to use your credit card on necessary life expenses. I know people who buy groceries with a credit card. Paying 18 or 24 or even 32 percent interest on milk and bread is not wise. I understand that people use credit cards for purchases they already have money for to get frequent flyer miles or reward points, and as long as you pay off the entire balance every month without interest, that can work. But using credit cards should be your choice—not something you're forced to do because you don't have money in reserve.

Sometimes, I'll counsel people about saving money, and they'll tell me, "But when I save money, I just turn around and spend it."

To that I reply, "Don't!" Saving does take discipline, but it's important.

Once you have that emergency cushion, begin planning how you're going to have a retirement account. Some people have 401k accounts where they work. Some teachers and preachers are eligible for a TSA (tax-sheltered annuity) that has certain advantages. Most people can also contribute to an IRA (individual retirement account). The advantage of these accounts is that you do not pay taxes on the money until you retire. Conversely, there is a Roth IRA. In this plan, you pay the taxes up front, but then when you take the money out, you do not pay taxes, regardless of how much the account increases. Whichever plan is best for you (you should find a trusted financial advisor to help you make the decision), start investing in your retirement now.

Another great investment is buying a home. The primary purpose of your home is for you to live in it and enjoy it. I counsel people to buy the nicest home they can reasonably afford. Your home is the only investment that can increase in value every day at the same time that it is being used every day. There are also great tax advantages to owning a house, especially if you make money when you sell it. As you decide what home to purchase, the needs of your family and how you can use it currently should be your biggest considerations, but also look at it as an investment potential.

After we had lived in a house for about seven years, a realtor came and asked if we would be willing to sell it. We did not have the house on the market, but when he told me what we might be able to sell it for, I got interested in selling. We had made some improvements and added on to the house, and we received nearly double what we originally paid.

Once we decided to sell the house, we began looking for a new place to live. I took into account the future value of homes in different neighborhoods. Ultimately, we bought some land and built a house. My biggest concern in looking for a new house was its location relative to the church where I pastor, but its appreciation value was also high on my list.

In your house search, consider the neighborhood as well. It is better to buy the worst house in the best neighborhood than the best house in the worst neighborhood. While it's tempting to try to maximize the house you can buy for the amount of money you have available, it will rarely prove to be a good long-term decision. Over time, neighborhoods tend to decline rather than improve. So starting in a neighborhood that is already on a downward trend is usually not the best choice.

Research with real estate agents, bankers, and on the internet to determine what is happening in the housing market in your area. Find out which parts of town are expected to be the most desirable in the future. Look at what style and size of houses people are building and buying. These will be major factors in determining the future value of your house when you decide to sell.

While a home can be a great investment, that's not its primary purpose. Its value in the future should be secondary to its use in the present. When we built our house, we wanted to have a "great room." We might have done that differently if we had been more focused on resale. But we expected to live there for years, and therefore we built the house to suit our lives.

Once you've made the big decision to buy a house to live in long-term, start thinking about what you can do to increase its value. This takes some discernment—not all investments are as valuable as another might be. Spending $40,000 on renovations does not necessarily mean that the value of your home will increase by an equal amount.

Do some research to find out which items will add the most value in the future. Some people have greatly increased the value of their house by painting it. Others have raised their property's value by adding on to the home.

Every area of the country differs in what innovation will add value and which will not. With that in mind, do your research. As a side note, don't just think you have to hire a contractor to improve your home. If you have skills and ability to do home improvement projects yourself, you can add a tremendous amount of "sweat equity" to the value of your house.

At some point, you may outgrow your home. One option you might consider that could increase your assets long-term is not reselling your home but refinancing it. Take the money that you have gained from the appreciation and buy another house. Then, you can rent out the first house and have someone else make the payments for you. Without taking any future money out of your pocket, you could potentially build equity in two homes instead of one. If you're willing to be a landlord, you will gain significant tax advantages (depreciation, an interest deduction, and so forth), and you will build your net worth.

Doing this successfully requires time on your part to learn what you are doing and very wise counsel from people familiar with your area, the current economy, and the particulars related to the contract. Although real estate is a great investment, it's far from risk-free, and you need to talk to people who have experience, such as reliable real estate agents and real estate investors. Be familiar with the risks and the rewards.

Not everyone has the mindset or the willingness to take the risks that are required for real estate investing. But there are a number of options for acquiring real estate that will produce an ongoing stream of income. Besides purchasing other properties to rent out, you could purchase properties to "flip," or fix up and sell. You could also purchase properties to sell on a "land contract" or rent-to-own basis.

Again, do not take any of these steps without spending time (a lot of time) learning the market in your area. Some people have nearly ruined themselves buying land or properties that they shouldn't have purchased. There are many opportunities in this area, but also many dangers. Proverbs 11:14 reminds us, "in the multitude of counsellors there is safety." Get counsel from many others and, above all, ask the Lord for wisdom.

If I reach the age where I am unable to work, I don't want to be a burden to others. If possible, I don't want my adult children to suddenly find they're strapped with my medical expenses. In fact, I want to be a blessing to them financially when I'm older. I want to leave an inheritance to them and my grandchildren.

As you go through life, ask yourself, "What am I doing to invest and prepare for the future?" Our desire should be not just to live for now, but to increase what God has given us. We should work to follow the wise servant's actions in Jesus' parable.

CONCLUSION

DO YOU NEED TO KILL A GIANT?

In the middle of battle, the Israelites were camped out on a hill, looking across to the Philistines. Basically, both sides had reached a stalemate. The Philistines and Israelites knew that to attempt crossing the valley between the hills would mean an immediate volley of stones and arrows from the other side. Both were stuck where they were.

Suddenly, trumpets blew as Goliath came out to shout his challenge to God's people. Standing more than nine feet tall, he towered over everyone else. No one was willing to risk his life against the giant. Even King Saul, who was a full head and shoulders taller than any of the other Israelites, refused to accept the challenge. I have to think that each day the words of Goliath became a little harsher and his insults grew a little more biting. In any case, no one was willing to stand against him.

No one, that is, until David arrived on the scene. Although he didn't know it at the time, God was planning on using David in a great way. Three of his brothers were in the army, and David's father Jesse sent him to deliver a care package and get an update on the battle.

After David arrived, Goliath came forth to issue his daily challenge, blaspheming the God of the Israelites. I can imagine David's expression of horror and indignation as he listened to the Philistine's words. Perhaps he expected Saul or one of the soldiers to do something about them. But no one did. All the trained men of war, the leaders, and even the king were fearful.

Maybe at that point David thought, *Well, if no one is going to kill this giant, I guess I'll have to.* Walking down to the valley, he picked up five stones and put one in his sling. Then, he marched forward to meet Goliath. Bravely, he killed the giant and won the battle. His faith in God carried him forward against a giant that no one else thought he could defeat.

All of us will face giants in life. Throughout this book, we've looked at some of the seasons of pressure in life that can easily become giants to us. We've looked at biblical ways to respond to things like grief, temptation, and money problems. Each of us will come to moments when we can either give up in defeat or, through faith, claim a great victory for God. No matter what the situation is that we're facing, we can kill those giants that come against us.

Let's look again at David's encounter with Goliath to uncover principles that will help us to live with victory through any season of pressure we may face.

Awakening to the Cause

David was not your battle-hardened soldier. In fact, he wasn't even part of the army, didn't intend to participate in the battle, and didn't have military equipment. He was literally just there to bring food to his brothers. But something happened in David's heart that turned him from a spectator to a soldier.

When David saw that swaggering soldier from the Philistine army make his boasts and insults against God and the Israelites, David grew indignant. He asked, "… who is this uncircumcised Philistine, that he should defy the armies of the living God?" (1 Samuel 17:26). David, this young shepherd boy, took a stand no one else was willing to take.

It's no secret that the world is an enemy of those who follow the Lord; it's been that way since the Fall. Jesus said, "If the world hate you, ye know that it hated me before it hated you" (John 15:18).

When the world attacks us for our beliefs, we should take action. We, like David, should be saddened if other Christians sit back, unwilling to stand up for what is right. The Israelites allowed their fear to intimidate them into backing down from Goliath. They had forgotten that God was on their side, and they didn't want to risk battle.

Sometimes, we are tempted to do exactly what the Israelites did. When our beliefs are attacked, it's tempting to back down and settle for a truce with the world. As more and more Christians step back from the battle, we can start to feel like we're alone.

But we're not alone. No matter how few Christians stand up for what is right, we have the Lord on our side. As a preacher once said, "You and God make a majority in any situation." Even if no one else is willing to stand up for what is right, we can because we have God with us. With the Lord on our side, nothing can prevent us from defeating our giant.

David was victorious over Goliath because he had the Lord. Although it seemed like everyone was against him, he did not let that deter him. And from his story, we hear him say incredible, convicting statements such as, "Is there not a cause?" and "The battle is the LORD's."

Let's go back to the beginning of the story and look at David's preparation. As he prepared for battle, he asked those around him, "What shall be done to the man that killeth this Philistine, and taketh away the reproach from Israel?" (1 Samuel 17:26).

This brings up an interesting point. We can fall into a mindset that getting earthly rewards on earth for standing up for what's right somehow detracts from our spirituality. But God put a reward system in place for serving Him.

God rewards us both on Earth and in Heaven for doing right. As David contemplated killing this giant, he wanted to know what to expect. He was told that he would have the king's daughter to marry and would never have to pay taxes. I don't know about you, but that sounds like a pretty good deal. Those rewards likely gave David an extra incentive to stand up to Goliath.

That's a comforting thought—God will take care of His people. While earthly rewards shouldn't be our first pursuit or only motive, God keeps a record of what we do for Him, even giving a cup of cold water in His name, to ensure that we will not be ignored or overlooked (Mark 9:41).

Accepting the Cause

David's mind was made up. Because of what he had heard and seen, he was ready to accept Goliath's challenge and take him in battle. Remember, the Israelites had been hearing this giant boast for forty days. They were literally stuck in a stalemate—unless someone did something, they had no idea how long they would stay on the hillside. You would think that they'd be glad someone was finally accepting the challenge, but that's not what happened.

You can rest assured that when you stand up to the pressure in your life—when instead of caving under it, you seek God's strength to live victoriously—not everyone around you will applaud that. When you, like David, accept the cause, others will, like the Israelites, add new layers of pressure.

When we accept a cause, people will question our motives. After David made his choice to stand up for what was right, his older brother antagonistically responded:

> *And Eliab his eldest brother heard when he spake unto the men; and Eliab's anger was kindled against David, and he said, Why camest thou down hither? and with whom hast thou left those few sheep in the wilderness? I know thy pride, and the naughtiness of thine heart; for thou art come down that thou mightest see the battle.*
> —1 SAMUEL 17:28

Can you hear the disdain in Eliab's voice? Here is David, his little brother—the lunch delivery boy—and he has the audacity to think that he can kill Goliath. From what we can gather from Scripture, Eliab had an impressive demeanor. In the previous chapter, when Samuel saw Eliab, he immediately assumed that he was the man chosen by God to be the next king of Israel (1 Samuel 16:6). You get this impression of a tall, strong soldier—a leader ready to attack Goliath head on. I can see the smirks and the eye rolls. "Oh please, David," he must have thought. "If I can't take Goliath on, you definitely can't." But David wasn't deterred.

Maybe you've experienced the reaction David got. It's one thing to be attacked by the world—it's quite another to have fellow Christians ridicule and discourage your decisions for God. As David learned, you're not going to get universal approval when you stand up to giants. I think that this, in part, stems from the fact that when others see you stand up to the pressure, they are embarrassed of and convicted over their lack of faith. They would rather have the giant win than see you triumph over the enemy they were unwilling and fearful to defeat.

When we accept a cause, people will criticize our methods. As David prepared for battle, his weapon of choice was his trusty slingshot. At his announcement, I have to wonder what the conversations would have been like in the armory.

"You can't be serious," one soldier might have said as he helped David. "Goliath carries a *spear*. The Philistines have swords and shields—this is the real deal, David. There's no way you can stand up to him with that slingshot."

Another one might have chimed in, "You've never been in a *real* battle before. If you're going to face the giant, at least let us help you get the right equipment."

In fact, Saul even offered to let him wear his armor. (I have to wonder: if Saul's armor was so good, why didn't Saul use it himself against Goliath? He was allowing David to fight using equipment he wasn't willing to use.) But because Saul was the tallest man in the kingdom, the armor didn't fit David. Finally, David decided enough was enough. He said, "I cannot go with these; for I have not proved them. And David put them off him" (1 Samuel 17:39).

David knew the slingshot worked. Even though it wasn't fancy, new, or impressive, David's attitude toward his weapons is a wonderful parallel to what our attitude should be toward the basic tools of the Christian life. Bible reading, memorization, prayer, soulwinning, and church attendance work. When people try to present new, unproven ideas to you, stick to the proven weapons of spiritual warfare. Keep on using what God has given you. Trust Him, rely on His Word, and go forward into battle.

When we accept a cause, people will compare our maturity. Saul looked down on David because he was a young man. He compared David's minimal experience to Goliath's experience and found it lacking. If you are willing to enter into the battle against your giant, people may say you aren't mature enough for the battle. But the truth is that people of every age face trials and giants. If you don't fight them when you are young, it doesn't get easier when you are older; it gets harder.

Whether you have been saved for three weeks or thirty years, God is the one who always wins the battle. As David said, "The battle is the LORD's" (1 Samuel 17:47). Don't listen to people who tell you that you can't find victory in seasons of pressure because you are too young or too inexperienced. When that happens, and it will, ask the Lord to help you block out those voices and claim the victory that only He can give.

Advancing the Cause

We know how David's encounter with Goliath ends—he experienced a monumental victory. But *David* didn't know what the ending would be as he stepped out to face Goliath. All he knew was that he had faith in a God who was much more powerful than any giant. We have that same God. When you, in faith, choose to follow God's Word even in seasons of pressure, even against the giants in your life, God is able and willing to give you the victory. Because David stood up to Goliath, the cause of Israel was advanced. And when you stand up to your giants, the cause of Christ is advanced.

A motivating factor behind David's decision to fight Goliath was to stop the shame and reproach brought on by the giant's insults. David was tired of no one standing up for right.

David knew that the primary focus of what was going on was not on him or on the rewards he could get. It was not only about getting revenge on Goliath's taunts. While that was part of the battle, there was something much bigger involved. This battle, as David knew, was all about God.

> *This day will the LORD deliver thee into mine hand; and I will smite thee, and take thine head from thee; and I will give the carcases of the host of the Philistines this day unto the fowls of the air, and to the wild beasts of the earth; that all the earth may know that there is a God in Israel. And all this assembly shall know that the LORD saveth not with sword and spear: for the battle is the LORD's, and he will give you into our hands.*—1 SAMUEL 17:46–47

The battles you face are an opportunity for God to be honored and glorified in your life. When you face trials and adversity with faith, you portray God in a positive light to others. God has called you to be an overcomer, and He doesn't leave you powerless in the battle. It is never God's plan for you to fight a battle on your own.

Remember the Battle of Jericho? Right before, Joshua had a meeting with the angel of the Lord. When Joshua asked whose side the angel was on, the angel replied, "...as captain of the host of the LORD am I now come" (Joshua 5:14). Joshua was not facing Jericho alone—he had God on his side.

The same thing that was true for David is true for us. God is willing and able to fight on your behalf. Whatever the giant is in your life, whatever the pressure point you feel you just cannot defeat, you can be victorious through God's power. David knew that God would deliver him from Goliath.

> *David said moreover, The LORD that delivered me out of the paw of the lion, and out of the paw of the bear, he will deliver me out of the hand of this Philistine. And Saul said unto David, Go, and the LORD be with thee.*—1 SAMUEL 17:37

David had seen God work on his behalf before to give him the victory over other enemies. When he was just a boy tending his father's sheep, David killed a bear and a lion that were threatening the flock. Looking back at the ways God has helped you before will build and strengthen *your* faith to trust Him for today's battles.

David knew that it was not his own strength that won his battles. He gave the credit to God. His belief that God could overcome any obstacle or enemy was in direct contrast to the belief of Saul and the army of Israel. Their view of God was small; David's was big. When we fail to have complete faith in God's promise of victory, we limit our view of Him.

David wasn't hesitant about his decision to fight. The Bible says, "David hastened, and ran toward the army to meet the Philistine" (1 Samuel 17:48). He knew that there was only one true God, and he recognized that the battle with Goliath was an opportunity to demonstrate that truth to every one who witnessed the battle, both Israelites and Philistines.

Halfhearted soldiers don't win battles. History is full of examples of smaller, less well-equipped armies that defeated superior enemies. During the Revolutionary War, the Continental Army never had the number of men or the weapons that the British had. Yet many of the British units were mercenaries fighting for money, while the Americans were fighting for their home and freedom. Our ragtag army, with God's help, won independence.

Over 150 years later, World War II was taking place. Winston Churchill was prime minister of England during those dark days. He encouraged his countrymen to continue the fight by saying, "We shall fight on the beaches. We shall fight on the landing grounds. We shall fight in the fields and in the streets. We shall fight in the hills. We shall never surrender!" To win spiritual battles, we must have that kind of commitment.

That's the attitude David had. When he stepped out in front of Goliath, he didn't waiver or wonder if God would *really* come through for him. Instead, he put his life on the line, took out his slingshot, and killed Goliath. He had total confidence in achieving victory.

When the battle was over, David not only killed Goliath, he cut off Goliath's head so there would be no doubt in anyone's mind. That's the kind of victory God wants you to win over every giant in your life.

With God's help and God's power, you *can* win the battles in your Christian life.

The Bible doesn't put the church of Jesus Christ on the defensive. Jesus said "And I say also unto thee, That thou art Peter, and upon this rock I will build my church; and the gates of hell shall not prevail against it" (Matthew 16:18). That means we are to be attacking the enemy, not running and hiding. Go toward the giants in your life in faith. You don't have to "hold on till Jesus comes." As Romans 8:37 says, we are "more than conquerors through him that loved us." You can win those battles now.

Almost three hundred years ago, the great hymn writer Isaac Watts penned these words. Let them be your song as you prepare to conquer your giants.

> *Am I a soldier of the cross,*
> *A follow'r of the Lamb?*
> *And shall I fear to own His cause,*
> *Or blush to speak His name?*

Must I be carried to the skies
On flow'ry beds of ease,
While others fought to win the prize,
And sailed through bloody seas?

Are there no foes for me to face?
Must I not stem the flood?
Is this vile world a friend to grace,
To help me on to God?

Sure I must fight if I would reign;
Increase my courage, Lord;
I'll bear the toil, endure the pain,
Supported by Thy Word.

Thy saints in all this glorious war
Shall conquer, though they die;
They see the triumph from afar,
By faith's discerning eye.

When that illustrious day shall rise,
And all Thy armies shine
In robes of vict'ry through the skies,
The glory shall be Thine.

All of us are going to face giants as we encounter seasons of pressure. At times, it will feel like insurmountable pressure. But God wants to win a victory in our lives. He doesn't want us to live in a constant state of defeat, buried under pressure and fear.

When the pressure is on, you can, through God's Word and in the strength of the Lord, rise to the challenge. God can and will work a victory in your life, just as He did in the life of David.

Visit us online

strivingtogether.com

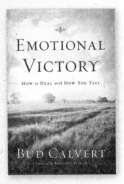
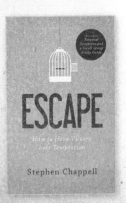